FLIGHT TO ALASKA-1930

Pilot Lombard (left), Co-Pilot Blodgett and Flit, Ready for Take-Off

FLIGHT TO ALASKA-1930

The Journal of Flit, an open cockpit biplane, and two young men who flew her from Boston to Alaska—and back again—for a holiday, in the earlier days of aviation.

LAURENCE M. LOMBARD

DEDICATED

to the young lady, who later became my wife, whose indifference at the time was more responsible for this trip than
she realized.

Editor's Note:

Airports were few and, when you could find one, often it was just a dusty field. You flew by the seat of your pants and you forecast the weather mostly by looking at the sky. Often, if your little craft began acting up, you landed in a farmer's field and fixed it yourself.

The year was 1930 and private flying was in its lively infancy. In the years since, flying has changed so dramatically that it's difficult to recall or imagine now what it was like then. But the story told here of a 1930 flight recaptures the feeling of those earlier days and the enthusiasm of the adventurous young men who lived them.

Laurence M. Lombard, a member of the Harvard class of 1917, is an attorney in Boston and makes his home in Dedham, Massachusetts. He wrote this account shortly after making the trip. In response to encouragement from friends, he is publishing it now with the thought that it will help show what flying for sport was like not so many years ago.

Table of Contents

Introduction

THE PRIVATE PLANE

UNTIL VERY RECENTLY the cost of owning a plane and the length of time taken to qualify as a pilot have militated against the private plane. I still believe private flying is very much in the development stage and that at least in 1930 and in New England with the rough country and changeable weather, it must be looked upon by most of us as a sport rather than a time-saving or dependable conveyance.

If the private plane owner wants to go from Boston to New York on business, it will save him time and trouble if he takes the midnight train over one night and back the next, rather than flying over in the average small plane. By the time he gets from the office to the airport, gets into his flying suit, checks the motor and takes off, forty minutes have been used up, granted that the plane was "on the line" with the engine warmed up when he arrived at the field. With many small planes it is necessary to stop at New Haven for gas, which will mean another thirty minutes. North Beach Airport, forty-five minutes from the Grand Central Station is the nearest approach to New York City, but landing, arranging for servicing and storing the plane and getting a taxi will take another thirty minutes. Thus our flier has spent two hours on the ground with virtually no gain toward his objective. If his flying time is no greater than his ground time, it will be a quick trip. This means at least four hours as against five hours on the train, with no allowance for the many little delays so familiar to all pilots.

But if I want to fly to New Haven for a football game, that is quite another matter. Unless it is a good day, I do not start. Then, under the urge of the big game, I dash from the office, climb quickly into the waiting plane; make a snappy landing at the New Haven airport, jump into a waiting taxi and arrive at the Yale Bowl within two hours after leaving the office, and only fifteen minutes late for the game. This is all very thrilling and I am quite in the spirit of a football game. The fact that it is too dark to take off after the game does not matter. My plane is not equipped for night flying, so I take the train to New York with friends. Also, the fact that it happens to be pouring on Monday morning when I planned to fly back to Boston does not matter, either. I take the morning train and arrive in Boston about noon. Two days later, with a favorable weather forecast, I take the evening train to New Haven and fly the plane home in the early morning. This was a pleasure trip, and time was not of the essence.

Nor did it matter, the following year that in flying to the Harvard-Yale game at New Haven, we ran into a thick fog bank between Providence and New Haven, and tried in vain to get through. We finally returned to the Providence airport and with three more fog-bound aviators drew up chairs in front of the radio at the field and formed our own enthusiastic cheering section.

Although the private plane is not always dependable as to time, it can be a tremendous source of pleasure, and I hope that the following account of our flight to Alaska will be of interest to sportsmen who may not yet have appreciated the possibilities which the private plane offers them. If the sportsman's holiday is to some island off the coast, or to an inland lake, hours or days may be saved in travelling by plane and the holiday has really commenced when the plane first takes to the air.

At the present time most private planes do not have the equipment, nor do most private pilots have the experience to make it safe for them to fly, regardless of the weather. But the small plane has already demonstrated its practicability and I anticipate tremendous advances in their safety and efficiency in the next few years.

MY EARLY FLYING

I am rather a new-comer in aviation. My first flight was at Hounslow, outside London, in the summer of 1918. I was on leave in England and Junius Richards, an Army friend arranged for me to have a "hop" at the British Training School. Apparently, my American Naval uniform was to the little English pilot what a red flag is to a bull. The take-off and landing were quite understandable, but most of my twenty minutes aloft were spent in my trying to locate either heaven or earth. Occasionally, the pilot would look back at me and smile and I did my best to return the courtesy.

In 1920 I circled the cathedral at Antwerp and had pointed out to me an Olympic swimming race that was said to be taking place in a small puddle below. My principal recollection of the flight is the anxiety I felt when, as we rose above the trees at the end of the field, our pilot took one hand off the controls to wave to a young lady in the upper window of a nearby house. But he was an ex-war pilot in the French air force and I consoled myself with the thought that at times he had probably weathered even greater dangers.

After these two flights my regard for the supermen who were able to conquer the air was nothing short of admiration, and I decided that flying was not for me.

Ten years later, in the spring of 1929, an old friend Alec Bright described his flying lessons to me. He had even ordered a plane. His enthusiasm was contagious. If he could do it, why couldn't I, and two days later I gave myself a birthday present of my first flying lesson.

I still remember vividly the awe with which I regarded the little Moth in which I was about to go aloft. I marvelled at the smallness of the propeller and the flimsy appearance of the entire plane. As nearly as I could remember there was very little difference between this ship and the Avro in which I had flown over London ten years before.

In order to take flying lessons it was necessary to pass a physical examination. I took the examinaton, but alas, without glasses my eyes could not meet the test and a certain vision was required without the aid of glasses. Before the next lesson my instructor asked me if I had taken the medical examination.

"Yep, yesterday afternoon," I replied, climbing quickly into the student's seat.

Fortunately no further questions were asked, and thereafter I was regarded as a regular student. The flying lessons fascinated me. When progress was slow, it served as a challenge to try harder, and every good day I reported for an early morning lesson before going to work. I was sure I should never be allowed to solo without the doctor's permit, but luck was with me. I soloed, and I had my ten hours of solo flying necessary before taking the test for a private pilot's license, without ever having to show the medical permit which I did not have.

To get a Federal license was impossible without the doctor's permit, but the Commonwealth of Massachusetts showed a more liberal attitude. On the recommendation of the same Army doctor who had failed to pass me for a Federal license, Massachusetts waived my "physical defect" and allowed me to take the flying test for a state license. Still there was one more hurdle. Practically all planes were registered by the Federal Government, and to fly a Federally licensed plane, a Federal pilot's license was required. What I needed was a plane registered only in Massachusetts. So in the fall of 1929 after eleven hours of solo flying I bought a Moth plane, named her "Flit" and registered her under the Commonwealth of Massachusetts. With a Massachusetts private pilot's license #26 in my pocket, and with "MASS. 36" painted on Flit's wings, at last I was beyond the pale of Federal jurisdiction, and could fly to my heart's content, unless, perchance, I ran afoul the hostile laws of some other state.

ALASKA—AN IDEA

Despite my limited license, a few week-end jaunts in Flit rapidly extended my geographic perspective. Although for a long time, I had wanted to see Alaska, until now the limitations of a lawyer's vacation had made the realization of this dream seem remote. Would it be possible to fly across the continent in Flit, put pontoons on her at Seattle and fly up the coast to Alaska?

At the suggestion of one of my law partners, Mr. Foye

Murphy, who had flown from Seattle to Skagway, Alaska, in a transport plane the previous summer, I wrote to Mr. J. L. Carman, Jr., President of the Alaska Washington Airways Company. This company, with headquarters at Seattle, had seaplanes based at several Alaskan ports and occasionally ran special trips from Seattle to Ketchikan, Juneau and Skagway. Mr. Carman replied that his pilots believed the trip from Seattle to Alaska would be possible in a Moth if I were in no particular hurry and were willing to wait for favorable weather; also his company would be glad to assist me in changing my plane from wheels to pontoons when I reached Seattle.

I

Pete and Preparations

"**H**ELLO!"

"Hello. Is this Pilot Lombard?"

"None other," I replied in some surprise. "Who are you?"

"This is Pilot Blodgett speaking and I have called up to offer my services as co-pilot from Boston to Alaska."

"What, Pete?"

"None other, yourself."

"Well, come up and talk it over."

Frederick N. Blodgett, better known as Pete, a young employee of The First National Bank of Boston, was an enthusiastic hunter and fisherman and an ideal companion on a camping trip, but I had never heard of Pete, the aviator.

"Do you know how to fly?" I inquired as he walked into the office.

"No, but I've been up two or three times, and I'd be glad to learn," he replied.

"Yes, I think you should have a few hours' instruction," I advised.

Although I had suggested this form of vacation to a number of friends, until now I had received no encouragement. Pete's enthusiasm was a happy contrast and as it was already early July we wasted no time in making definite plans. It was finally agreed that Pete would begin taking flying lessons immediately and I should get the plane ready to leave in about a month.

Flit was a small, open cockpit, two-seater biplane, with one seat in back of the other. She could be fitted with dual controls, although all the instruments were in the rear cockpit or regular flying seat. She was fitted with an English De Havilland Gipsy, four cylinder, eighty horsepower engine.

1

I had had the plane streamlined in order to increase the speed, so that she had a cruising speed of about eighty miles an hour and a top speed of ninety-five. In preparation for the trip, an extra gas tank had also been installed in the front cockpit, giving a total cruising radius of around 400 miles.

With Pete as an assured co-pilot, I now bought a pair of second hand Edo pontoons and, after trying a couple of landings on the water, flew down to my parents' summer place at Hyannisport for the weekend. It was my first experience flying off the water, but it was so easy and Flit behaved so beautifully that I immediately had the pontoons removed, crated and shipped to Seattle to await our arrival.

Pete sent out a 30-06 Springfield government rifle, we wrote several friends scattered across the country warning them of our approach and we really seemed to be making progress. We confided our proposed trip to a few local friends, but failed to receive much support. Their comments were not such as to create overconfidence and often they declined to take us seriously. Appreciating the fact that a slight miscalculation in landing or taking off might terminate our trip at an early date, and not wishing to have too many people laugh at us, we decided to drop further mention of our destination. We changed our expressed plans to those of a scientific expedition west for the purpose of collecting statistics. Science seemed to be the accepted motive of all modern adventures, so the lofty ideals of our journey could no longer be questioned.

Pete was an enthusiastic hunter and I was an enthusiastic aviator; so Pete hoped ultimately to discover if the Kodiak bear were as difficult to kill as reported; and I wanted to know if two amateurs could take a small Moth plane over the mountains and up to Alaska.

We feel our vacation has answered both of these questions in the affirmative and this is our real contribution to the cause of science. Our scientific note book is filled with valuable observations but, as these would appear more appropriately in a purely scientific treatise, I shall only quote a few of them here:

"There are 143 golf courses (not counting Tom Thumb) on the air line between Cleveland, Ohio, and Des Moines, Iowa, whereas there are only 98 baseball diamonds and 56 race tracks."

"Bicycle races are held on Sunday in Ohio and it is perfectly feasible to enjoy a race from an altitude of 1000 feet provided the pilot does not become too engrossed in the race—as mine did."

"Des Moines, Iowa, has the most elaborate filling stations in the United States."

"As the United States Government strip maps are by far the best aviation maps in this country and cost only 40¢ a map, they are not obtainable at any airports in the United States at which we inquired, with the exception of the emergency field at Redding, Oregon. Here they very kindly loaned us their only strip map for going over the mountains."

When we took off on the afternoon of August 17th 1930, Pete had completed a little over five hours' instruction and had soloed twice although he had never flown a Moth. I had about 150 hours of flying and all but 10 of it had been in my Moth. Neither of us pretended to know anything about the engine which had just been overhauled.

We planned to take it easy across the continent, occasionally stopping off to see friends as, in addition to being a scientific expedition, this was our vacation. Sitting in a small, open cockpit plane for more than seven hours a day is far from restful. At a cruising speed of 80 miles an hour we figured that if we averaged 500 miles a day we should be doing well, considering the country we must cross and the head winds we were likely to meet.

II

The Start

W E HAD HOPED to get away late Friday afternoon, but storms, delay in fitting a new steel propeller and a last minute leak in our main gas tank (located in the upper wing directly over the cockpit) held us up until Sunday. Early Sunday afternoon all was ready except the packing. Each of us arrived at the field with what he considered the minimum equipment possible for making such a trip. Our stowage space consisted of a compartment about the size of a large suit case, located in the fuselage just behind the rear cockpit. Extending aft from this, inside the fuselage were two long canvas pockets I had had installed for carrying golf clubs. In these we stowed fishing rods, a .22 rifle, stakes and rope for tying down the plane, canvas covers for the engine and cockpits, a spare strip of fabric and some dope for repairing the wings and these pockets were full. Each of us was to sit on a parachute. This left our baggage compartment free to carry tools, strip maps of the route to Seattle (except for 300 miles over the mountains for which we had been unable to obtain maps) a can of grease and a can of oil, a few spare motor parts, such as spark plugs, springs, washers, gaskets, cotter pins, screws and wire, a first aid kit, respectable clothes for social life and warm clothes for high altitudes and Alaska.

My "warm clothes" were a wonderful fur lined balloonist suit given me by my friend Donald Hood, which he had worn in World War I. He and his wife Alva also gave me a small leather bound notebook, inscribed in gold lettering "Log of Flit," in which I kept the original notes of our trip.

There wasn't one quarter enough space for our minimum clothing requirements, so Pete boldly set to work eliminat-

4

ing my luggage while I discarded his. We combined toilet kits avoiding duplication of all but tooth brushes and left out nonessentials such as pyjamas. In the end we allowed each other, in addition to flying clothes, one business suit, one necktie, one collapsible hat and one complete change. These were jammed into one parachute bag, which in turn was jammed into the compartment. Other clothes would have to be bought and discarded along the way.

Even so, the East Coast mechanics who had just completed overhauling the engine wondered if we would be able to take off with such an overloaded plane. They had done a good job, however, and about three o'clock Sunday afternoon, August 17, 1930, the sawed-off Faery Reed steel propeller which we had just borrowed from Skyways Company pulled us off the ground at the East Boston Airport; we waved good-bye to Pete's brother and sister-in-law who had patiently stood by for two days to see us off and Flit's nose headed west.

Circling two thunderstorms in the Berkshires gave us a little sport for the first afternoon, then as we were passing over Troy at 7500 feet, Pete informed me that a piece of metal on the top of the cowling was flapping in the breeze.

"Keep your head down in case it lets go," I yelled through the voice tube, as I throttled down the motor and put our nose down in a gradual glide toward Schenectady. I was afraid to dive too rapidly for fear the metal might give way and tear a hole in a wing or go through the gas tank overhead. We were keeping our heads well below the windshields when there was a sudden "whist" and the disturbing piece of metal flashed overhead and started its descent in the general direction of New York's Executive Mansion. I hope it reached the ground without human interference.

We circled the field at Schenectady. The wind was light from the northwest. I flattened out a few feet above the ground and the overloaded plane dropped in a horrible landing. Pete looked quizzically at me. I allowed that I sometimes did better and quickly got out to inspect our undercarriage. With this only our first landing how could we expect Flit to last across the continent? But no harm was done, and we looked in vain to see whence the missing piece of metal had come. Accustomed to driving Fords, we decided it was probably just an unnecessary spare part, so prepared to leave.

The field at Schenectady was lined with autos and spectators, a Sunday crowd out to see a parachute jump. Never having seen one except in the movies, I too was curious. We saw the unfortunate jumper twice climb out on the wings of the plane, then lose his nerve; and the plane landed that he might be given another fight talk. Although our sympathies were with the jumper, we could not wait to see the outcome.

As he climbed into the front cockpit, Pete inquired a little shyly where we were.

"This is the village of Schenectady. And that little building," I added a moment later as we rose over the river, "is the General Electric plant."

It takes a little time to develop one's perspective in cross-country flying, but after a few days Pete was spotting the airports before I was.

III

Experience: Syracuse to Iowa City

THE SCENE was the Syracuse airport, Monday morning, August 18th, at 8:30 a.m., the second day of our trip. I was in the cockpit; the field mechanic was at the "prop."

"Switch off, throttle closed," he called.

"Switch off, throttle closed," I echoed.

He turned her over once. "Switch off, throttle closed," he called again, and again I repeated.

He gave her a turn and away went the engine, but fortunately the throttle had been closed and he was standing properly clear of the propeller, so no one was hurt. The mechanic looked at me queerly, and I motioned him to the cockpit and pointed at the switches. They were both off, and the engine was running serenely.

We shut off the gas to stop the engine and investigated. The ground wire had become disconnected so the switches which were supposed to short circuit the magnetos had no effect. Here was a good lesson for us. If the throttle had been open, as it well might have been for sucking gas into the carburetor before starting in the morning, the plane might have charged ahead over the blocks and seriously injured the man cranking. After this I invariably tested both switches each time before stopping the motor. Also thereafter we always stood in back of the prop when turning her over.

Cleveland by two o'clock gave us a short day with an afternoon of golf and a visit with my sister and brother-in-law, the Robert Groves and their family.

On the following day from Cleveland to Des Moines

7

we had all the flying we wanted. There is a long stretch of flat country across Ohio and Illinois and near Lake Michigan the cold air from the lake striking the warmer air over the land tends to make it bumpy. We took on a full load of gas at Toledo and soon after leaving the field a strong smell of gas told us our extra tank was leaking. This tank was located in the front cockpit about in Pete's lap. Pete thought the leak was in the middle seam of the tank. It was dripping directly between his legs and, although it was evaporating almost as soon as it landed on the cockpit floor, we did not like the situation and decided to land.

Going back to Toledo would have used up an hour so with flat country all around we picked a big field and put down in it. After pumping about five gallons out of this extra tank into the main tank in our upper wing, the leak seemed to stop and we continued toward Chicago.

For lunch we landed at the Ford Field at Lansing, Illinois, about thirty miles south of Chicago. After circling the field, true to my New England training, I aimed short of the circle in the middle of the field. Misjudging the size of the field, we rolled to a stop long before reaching the circle. The hangar was at the far end of the field. Pete wanted exercise so dismounted and ran to the hangar. Not to be beaten, I gave her the gun, took to the air for a few hundred yards and landed again before reaching the hangar. The field was almost a mile square, and we had landed three quarters of a mile from the hangar. We New Englanders have much to learn about the size of airports in our United States.

We did not get away from Lansing Field until 4:30 p.m. Chicago time. Des Moines before night seemed an ambitious hope but as we left the smoky atmosphere around Chicago flying conditions were ideal. The air was smooth, the country was flat and, by flying at only 800 feet altitude to increase our speed, we were rapidly dropping the miles behind us. Already I considered Pete a master pilot and except for occasional checks on the towns and the clock, I spent most of my time reading *All Quiet on the Western Front.*

Above the prison at Joliet we left the railroad and set

a course due west for Davenport, Iowa. All through the middle west the country is laid out in sections, large squares, with the boundaries running north and south, and east and west. The borders of the sections are distinctly marked by fences and in many places, by roads. Navigating is thus made very simple, with the principal danger that of falling asleep from the monotony of following a straight line across the country. We covered the 160 miles from Lansing to Davenport at the rate of ninety miles an hour. After crossing the Mississippi, I looked in vain for the Davenport Airport. There was a military field across the river at Moline and another field at Rock Island, but once having crossed into Iowa, we disliked giving up our gain, our third state that day, so we pushed on to Iowa City sixty miles beyond. Having maintained our speed, in another forty minutes we were on the ground at the new municipal airport at Iowa City.

IV

Our First Night Flight

SINCE LEAVING CHICAGO we had gained an hour on the clocks, so it was only six. The attendant at the hangar assured us we would have daylight until after 7:30 and said we could easily land any time before eight o'clock. Refueling usually kills the better part of an hour, but this was a race against darkness and within half an hour we were supplied with gas and oil and were ready to take off for Des Moines, 105 miles away.

The hangar was at the edge of the field. After taking on gas, we taxied across the cement apron in front of the hangar out onto the field. Taxiing a little to one side so as not to fill the hangar with dust when we "gave her the gun" and heading Flit's nose directly into the sun, I opened the throttle wide and pushed the control stick forward. The motor roared, and we gained speed. Our tail lifted until in flying position, and we sped lightly over the smooth field. I gradually eased the stick back until with a light touch of the fingers on the stick, I could feel Flit was ready to fly. Slowly I pulled the stick back toward my stomach; the ground dropped away, and as we climbed steadily in the smooth air, we seemed more related to the sun and its world than to the earth.

It was a beautiful evening and the gently rolling country which had replaced the flat fields looked green and fresh, with only an occasional brown crop to remind us of the dry summer. The sun reddened as it approached the horizon and after twenty-five minutes when we were still less than half way to Des Moines, a cloud bank rose up to meet the sun. It was a dramatic sight as the sun dropped crimson below the many colored clouds, and the country under-

10

neath seemed to take on fantastic shades of blue and purple—dramatic, yes, but we were not quite ready for this display of nature's drama. A few lights came on in the towns below and seemed to wink at us as we flashed by. Still at an altitude of only 800 feet and with our motor turning up a flat 2000 revolutions, we were speeding along at 95 miles an hour according to our air speed indicator. Unfortunately, this indicator was on the strut almost at the end of the wing. It was barely visible in the fading light, and in a few minutes our speed would be purely guesswork. Far ahead and to our right a bright light flashed—the beacon at Grinnell. That was forty miles from Des Moines. Should we land there at the emergency field or should we go on the forty miles? There was another bright flashing light ahead.

"That must be the beacon at Newton, only twenty miles from Des Moines."

As we could still see the ground, we decided to push on to Newton. It seemed to be brightening up a little ahead.

"If the clouds would only break and give us a few minutes more of daylight!"

It looked like rain for the morrow and we preferred to spend the day at Des Moines. Thus by postponing the issue we led ourselves into it, and darkness came upon us with a vengeance.

Again I looked out at the air speed indicator, but it was just a faint outline and quite indistinguishable. This gave me a little start and I looked quickly at the instrument board. While watching the lights ahead and below, I had failed to notice how dark it was around the plane. The various dials were barely discernible. I moved the control stick and banked slightly, but it was too dark to see the effect on the bank indicator. There were no lights on the instrument board, and my only flashlight was safely out of reach in the baggage compartment behind my cockpit. Although I had been a passenger at night in commercial planes, I had never piloted after dark before. I cannot say that I was pleased as I contemplated our situation, but mingled with an appreciation of our foolishness was a distinct thrill at the challenge presented. I loosened my safety belt and rose slightly in the seat to change my position, not that I was uncomfortable but I wanted to feel sure I was alert and ready to act quickly. Reaching for the throttle, I closed it and then opened it again to make sure it was free and to keep my ears sensitive to the sound of the motor.

The beacon at Newton flashed brilliantly ahead and on the same line we gradually made out two more flashing lights. "The second must be Des Moines."

The ground was now a dark haze. Only by the farm house lights could we guess our altitude. Watching the horizon and the lights ahead, I pushed the right foot pedal, giving right rudder and banked slightly, then reversed and banked slightly to the left. Holding the stick lightly in my fingers, I pulled the nose up a little, then forced the stick forward, dipping the nose. These motions gave me confidence in the darkness.

"Men have landed safely before, in the dark," I thought, "and after all, landing lights don't help much—if they will only give us the flood lights."

I exaggerated all the banks and turns. "Just to get the feel," I called to Pete.

A subdued "OK," was his only answer.

Then I throttled the motor, dipped the nose and slipped sharply for a few seconds. The wires sang shrilly, almost screamed in the darkness. It was a weird sensation. We might very well have to slip in when landing, and there was no harm in knowing how it felt and how it sounded. These manouevres completed, I opened the throttle to what sounded right and steadied the plane on a course for the beacons and Des Moines. Life seemed brighter now and I sat back once more to enjoy the flight. With the short stack of our exhaust belching a steady stream of red and purple fire as the only light on Flit we roared on through the darkness. Although I knew we were not up over 1000 feet, the stars seemed to have closed in around us and appeared quite as near as the lights on the ground.

The boundary lights were on at Newton as we flew over the beacon. Even with this to help us land, it was dark now and we did have plenty of gas to make Des Moines; it was only twenty miles away, and they might put on the flood lights for us there—and if we were going to crack up on our first night landing, we might as well do it at a real airport. Intoxicated by the thrill of the night flight, we decided to continue. As long as we were flying we felt safe—perhaps we only wanted to delay the evil moment of our landing.

The lights of Des Moines soon took shape. There was a row of evenly spaced lights! "They must mark the airport. Yes—or is that the state fair grounds we saw advertised at the Iowa City Airport?" We circled three times at a low altitude and even zoomed the field as much as we dared to attract attention. The roar of our motor was heard, the flood lights flashed on and we slipped in over a row of red lights which we later discovered marked a row of telegraph poles.

I for one gave a sigh of relief as our wheels and tail skid touched the ground and we came to a stop safely within the lighted area. Night flying is now common practice for mail and transport pilots the world over, but the first night flight in our little plane, unequipped with flying lights, over strange country and into a strange field with nothing to show us the direction of the wind, gave us quite a scare. We agreed to be more careful in estimating daylight in the future.

V

More Middle West

As IT WAS RAINING the next morning, we were undecided about leaving until a U. S. Army Boeing fighter came in from Chicago, refueled and was off again, bound west. That settled it. If they could do it so could we, and in that flat country we figured we could land Flit in almost any field. So we were soon improving our complexions with rain drops at the rate of eighty miles an hour.

While scooting between two thunderstorms which seemed determined to shut off our view, we passed over the town of Wahoo in a downpour of rain. I announced the name of the town to Pete through the voice tube. Had I entertained any doubts as to Pete's college affiliations prior to this time, the Dartmouth Wahoo cheer which issued forth from the forward cockpit would have settled the matter. The inhabitants of Wahoo must have thought the advance Dartmouth guard for the Southern California game was making an early trip west.

At Omaha, Nebraska, we had our spare gas tank soldered. From Omaha to North Platte, Wyoming, the land began to rise. It would have been easy to follow the Union Pacific tracks which took a turn to the southward and then came up the river valley in a northwesterly direction to North Platte, but North Platte was directly west from Omaha, so we decided to follow a compass course. By so doing we felt we could not get lost, as other railroad tracks came down from the north to North Platte. At first it was easy to follow the section lines. But as the country became sparsely populated and the terrain was rougher, the roads wound around the hills following the course of least resistance and the section lines disappeared. So over the Wyoming prairies and bad

14

lands we found ourselves flying a compass course fully fifty miles from the railroad tracks and at times probably even farther away from the nearest ranch or farmhouse. It was rough, unfriendly country but if we were going to cross the mountains, we had to get accustomed to this. There were occasional spots where we might have landed, but we hoped we should not have to—and we did not. After our 200 miles across country, the Union Pacific tracks were a welcome sight as they bore up from the south.

The field at North Platte is on the north bank of the Platte River, east of the town. We circled the field and came in over the river into a light westerly breeze. The field is about 3,000 feet above sea level but hardly high enough to notice any difference in landing.

We taxied Flit up to the gas tank beside a little Aeronca. The Aeronca is a high winged monoplane, with a small two-cycle engine, really little more than a power glider large enough for one person, with a quick take off and a slow landing speed. The pilot who had the agency for the Aeronca planes in that territory told us he had sold three of them in the previous two weeks. The ranchers buy them for running their fences, for with a plane they are able to accomplish in a morning what otherwise would take them a week.

"If they can ride a horse, they can ride one of these things," the pilot said as he fitted himself into the little cockpit.

The Wyoming ranchers examining their fences by airplane, landing between sage bushes, making repairs and returning to the ranch house for lunch! What next?

VI

Another Lesson

AS WE WATCHED the Aeronca float away to the eastward, our attention was attracted by the roar of a trimotor, the big Boeing transport coming in from Cheyenne. We watched her bank gracefully over the hangar and circle to start her glide. The wind was still from the west as in our landing a few minutes earlier. Pete ran out to the river bank to get a movie and I joined him with the still camera. She floated in, but seemed to glide forever. Pete looked up at the wind sock.

"Look, the wind's shifted," he cried, and sure enough, there was the wind sock blowing straight out towards the west. The Boeing touched the ground in what appeared to be a perfect three-point landing. It looked as though the pilot were going to get away with it. Suddenly the wind caught her tail, the large ship swung around, headed straight for us and the river. As she completed her ground loop, her right wheel buckled and she collapsed like a stricken bird, on her right wing. The right undercarriage, lower right wing and all the supporting struts were demolished.

This lesson certainly taught us what a slight change in wind can do to a landing and how quickly the winds shift, even in relatively flat open country. In the future, we were even more careful than heretofore to observe the exact direction of the wind at the moment of landing or taking off.

It seemed a tough break for the pilot. What more could he have done? We talked with him after the accident. He had no alibi to offer and gave no excuses. While flying on to Cheyenne that afternoon, 210 miles distant, we met two more Boeing trimotors, one coming out to take the passengers

16

on to Des Moines and Chicago and the other bringing company officials to investigate the accident. We stopped off at Cheyenne and went to see the Boeing manager to give him our story, how the wind had shifted after the pilot had started his glide and how we had taken a motion picture of the entire incident. The pilot's story had seemed a hard one for the company to swallow, but it was true. I hope the company believed us and that the pilot kept his job.

Cheyenne, Wyoming, is 6200 feet above sea level. As we approached, flying about 2000 feet above the ground, we could see the miniature village squatting alone in the flat, open prairies. High mountain ranges loomed against the horizon to the north; occasional peaks rose to the south, and still more mountains rising abruptly behind the city formed the western background for Cheyenne.

During our trip west, doubting friends had questioned our ability to clear the mountains in our little ship. To try Flit out in the Rockies was one of the purposes of the trip. Once with Maryan Freyter,* former Army flier, as ballast I had made 10,000 feet in a test hop at East Boston, but that was the highest I had ever attempted. After leaving Cheyenne, we were to have mountains with a vengeance so we decided to "try her out." I pointed her nose upward, gave her the gun and we climbed in a gradual climbing turn for half an hour until our altimeter showed 12,000 feet above sea level. To be sure we had only half a load of gas, but we had not reached our limit and might have gone higher had it not been so cold. We should certainly have to wear all our clothes for the mountain hops and I was grateful for Don Hood's fur lined balloonist suit. "At any rate this looks encouraging," we thought, as we spiralled down 6000 feet to the diminutive Wyoming capital, "12,000 feet ought to get us through almost any mountain pass."

---

* Freyter was formerly Chief Mechanic at Skyways and subsequently a mechanic at East Coast Aircraft Corporation. He was a careful pilot and an ever willing helper. Two days before Christmas, when flying home to see his family, his plane went into a tail spin almost over his own home, crashed and he was killed—one of those unfortunate accidents that are very difficult to explain.

At Cheyenne while having our oil changed, we studied our maps with the mail pilots. It was sure to be bumpy over the passes into Salt Lake City, but if we could make 12,000 feet, we ought to clear the worst bumps, they advised us. If we could only reach the highest mountains in the early morning air it would not be so bad, but in the middle of the day after the sun is up the currents through the mountain passes are always rough. The pilots further advised us that if in the mountain passes we found ourselves in a down current and unable to gain altitude, we might head over toward the face of the mountain and get upward current always rising there. During the night the atmosphere is cooled and becomes of even tempeature throughout. This makes flying smooth in the early morning. The heat of the sun causes uneven temperatures and wind currents which get worse as the day goes on. By late afternoon the air is again sufficiently cool to make flying noticeably smoother. This is true over all kinds of country, particularly where there is a wide variation of temperature between night and day.

We had hoped to spend the night at Cheyenne but the hop over the mountains into Salt Lake City would be strenuous enough for one day. In order to get over the worst of the mountains as early in the morning as possible, we decided to push on to Parco that night. The pilots had some doubts as to whether we could get off the field at Parco, 7700 feet above sea level, but they said it was a large field and, because of the way Flit had performed to date in the higher altitudes, we decided to make a try. We had been gradually eliminating extra weight as we came along. Our change of clothing had gone overboard and at Des Moines we had left the maps of territory which we had already covered. It might be necessary to leave our respectable clothes and rifle, Pete might have to walk, but somehow Flit was going to clear those far-famed mountains separating us from Great Salt Lake and forming the Continental Divide.

VII

Our First Mountains

IT WAS 5:30 IN THE AFTERNOON when we left Cheyenne, but it was a beautiful clear evening and the weather reports ahead were favorable. Beyond Cheyenne we followed the Union Pacific tracks due west toward the Laramie Mountains. We climbed steadily, but could not climb fast enough for the rising country and had to head back to get altitude. I tried our newly acquired theory and headed south toward the face of a high plateau. The theory worked and as we closed on the wall of rich brown rock we struck an up-current of air. Flit rose steadily and with increased altitude we again headed for the pass to the westward. There was a Union Pacific train winding up the canyon below. While we were trying to gain our altitude, it held its own with us and even went ahead.

The country below became rugged and the possibility of a safe landing looked remote. The railroad track at the bottom of the canyon was the only possible place where one could hope to land a plane. In the pass we felt our first "mountain bumps" but we were soon to find that, comparatively speaking, these were really caused by the cool smooth air of late afternoon and should not be classed as mountain bumps at all.

As we climbed into the Laramie Mountains we experienced our first sensations of danger from engine trouble. I noticed a strange throb, quite regular, as when the occupant of one train hears another pass in the opposite direction. Until now our motor had behaved perfectly. Here in our first real mountains it had decided to give trouble! I became somewhat excited and the throb seemed more frequent. I listened intently and it ceased. Then it

19

went on again as regularly as before. Although Pete did not notice anything, I was sure this was not my imagination.

"Should we continue to Parco or put back to Cheyenne where there are good mechanics?" I wondered. Then I discovered the cause of the throb. To fortify myself for the mountain trip, I had bought some chewing gum. With each operation of the jaws the sound of the motor's vibration in my ears had changed. As I became excited, I chewed more rapidly; and as I listened intently, I stopped chewing. With a feeling of distinct relief I made the necessary repairs to the motor by blowing out the chewing gum behind the first range of the Laramie Mountains. Not every pilot can repair his motor while still in the air.

At 10,000 feet we cleared the pass with 1000 feet to spare. We followed the ridge of the mountain to the north, and while the toy-like Union Pacific train wound its snakey course along the steady grades, we jumped ahead over gorges and ridges in a dash for the Lincoln Highway out ahead.

Behind the Laramie Mountains we passed near the famous wool town of the same name. The country underneath was mountainous and desolate but there were occasional plateaus and most of the way we kept within gliding distance of the Lincoln Highway, thinking we might land there if necessary.

The sun was setting as we passed low over Parco. A group of large oil tanks and one block of modern buildings with a pretty little garden between the buildings and the railroad tracks comprised the city as we saw it. Out beyond the oil tanks was the airport, a large flat field with a small shack and wind sock at one corner.

As Rawlins, seven miles beyond, was a larger town according to our map and had a landing field, we pushed on. But Rawlins turned out to be a mining town nestled below a small range of mountains. Should the wind have come from the north or west, we would have had to take off toward the mountains and with climbing such a slow process in those high altitudes we should have had to bank steeply while flying low over the ground. We put back and landed at the less inviting town of Parco.

With our altimeter reading 7800 feet above sea level,

we came in fast with very little wind. The field would hardly be called smooth but it is large and, except for scaring up a few rabbits, we had no trouble with our landing. Two boys on duty at the shack came out to meet us. They asked if ours was the plane coming through from Cheyenne then read our number and seemed to know all about us. This was an emergency Boeing field with a man on duty night and day. In this rugged country the departure and arrival of all planes are "put on the tape." As soon as we left Cheyenne we had been "put on the tape" and the ticker service reported us to all fields along the route as "small biplane M137 westbound leaving Cheyenne 5:30." Upon our arrival at Parco the boy on duty ran back to the shack and "put us on the tape" again so Cheyenne and other stations knew we were safely down for the night.

We staked the plane down and one of the boys motored us to town in the usual dilapidated Ford. "Wings" was being shown at the movies in Rawlins that evening and we agreed to meet our driver after dinner and "take in the show." We were surprised to find a thoroughly modern hotel at Parco. The explanation was that Parco is a regular stopping place for tourists motoring east and west along the Lincoln Highway. By the time we had had baths and dinner we realized that 600 miles in eight hours' flying time was a good day's work and that a bed was far more attractive than any moving picture.

VIII

The Wasatch Range

THE NEXT MORNING we were greeted with a slight leak in our main gasoline tank in the upper wing. It was not serious and would certainly hold for the 100 odd miles to Rock Springs where there was a regular Boeing field with mechanics. The idea of going over the Wasatch Mountains with a leaking gas tank did not appeal to us and we were glad of the chance of a thorough inspection at Rock Springs.

In order to save weight we did not take on any gas at Parco, deciding that we could reach Rock Springs with the half tankful we had left in our main tank. To lighten the ship still more, I presented the boys at the field with *All Quiet on the Western Front*. I had almost finished it and from the appearance of the country I doubted that I should do much reading during the next few days. After chasing a few wild horses from the field sharply at 6:30 a.m. we "gave her the gun" and were delighted to see how well Flit took off at the high altitude. To get off the ground required quite a long run and several bounces but once in the air we climbed slowly but steadily. Before banking, I kept straight ahead into the light wind until 500 feet above the ground. Just as we saw the sun rising behind a distant mountain in the east we swung back on our course and passed so low over the garden in front of our hotel that Pete was able to censure me for having failed to shut the window in our bedroom.

Rawlins looked picturesque in the rosy light of early morning. The airport and part of the city were still obscured by the morning mist. Had we landed there, we should still be on the ground.

The way into Rock Springs was mountainous and interesting but most of the time we were able to keep within gliding distance of the Lincoln Highway. This highway was not built as a landing field but one or two planes have landed on it with safety in places. Compared with most of the surrounding country, the narrow strip of winding roadway looked like paradise.

Rock Springs is situated between three small mountain ranges and is at the junction of several creeks. The field is north of the town almost under a high overhanging plateau and is subject to very tricky and shifty wind currents. We were careful to circle the town at a fair altitude before coming in on a long glide to the field.

The Boeing mechanics were busy taking the motors out of a trimotor that had nosed over in the take-off a few days before. A wheel had given way, probably when she struck a soft spot at the edge of the field where it was muddy from heavy rains. No one was hurt but the plane had to be completely taken down and put together again. Each day we were having impressed upon us the importance of being careful in our landings and take-offs.

The chief mechanic was glad to look at the leak in our gas tank. It was a very slight leak in the trailing edge of the tank, the same thing we had had just before leaving Boston and which Maryan Freyter had assured us would probably cause us trouble throughout the trip. The mechanic thought it would hold until we reached Salt Lake City, although of course that was just a guess. We decided to save the strain on the main tank by using it only half full and filling our emergency tank. This would give us plenty of margin for the flight to Salt Lake City. It was less than 200 miles but the mountains were really high and there was plenty of opportunity to get lost if we happened to follow the wrong valley. The weather report was propitious, although beyond Salt Lake City the weather was unsettled. It was still only 8:30 a.m. so we decided to hurry on before midday when the air in the mountains became worse.

After leaving Rock Springs, there was no doubt but that the mountains over which we were now flying were different from anything we had yet encountered. The railroad tracks and the Lincoln Highway gave us small consolation now as they wound through the narrow gorge below, and at times our course took us far away from both. After clearing one range, we always found a higher range ahead, and in all directions, as far as the eye could see there was an ocean of beautiful peaks.

As we climbed slowly up one canyon at about 10,000 feet, far above us and above the passes through which we were slowly struggling, we saw one of the Boeing trimotors like some great eagle sailing steadily on toward the west.

We climbed and climbed but somehow the air in the mountain passes did not seem to have the same buoyancy it had over Cheyenne. Up we would go for two or three hundred feet; then striking a bump or a down-current of air, we would lose our last five minutes worth of climbing. Occasionally we would swing back and climb toward the face of one of the overhanging mountains to get the benefit of the lift from the up-current near the face and top of the mountains. In the middle of the passes the winds often seemed to sweep in from the slopes on either side and meet in strong down-currents of very bumpy air. We tried to get above these currents.

Slowly we gained our altitude until we were flying at between 11,000 and 12,000 feet. This was almost Flit's ceiling and at such an altitude, we could only make about sixty miles an hour. Looking down at the rugged walls of the valley, we seemed almost stationary. To save time we cut corners and even left the winding railroad tracks. Little help they could be to us in that country if we were forced to land!

Crossing one knife-like ridge with less than 500 feet to spare, we were confronted with a gorgeous panorama of red-brown ridges and peaks. Below were two long canyons diverging from us in a general westerly direction. Which should we follow? The left hand valley looked the more inviting. It seemed to be ever widening and might be a pass through to the high mountains beyond. But this was no time for guess work. A slight miscalculation might lead us far from our course and valleys where a plane might land were few and far between.

A brief sea training had taught me not to doubt my compass without sufficient cause. We chose the narrow right hand valley, though not without misgivings. Keeping close to the mountains at the canyon side, we got the benefit of the up-current of air. The walls of the canyon were of rich red rock, for we had now passed the tree zone. From the left a deep ravine cut transversely into the rock wall. Passing close to it, Pete tried to take a picture, but the air was so rough it was almost impossible to hold onto the camera.

Beyond the pass for which we were aiming we could see the black clouds of a thunderstorm encircling a high peak. "If only Flit would go faster!"

But we were already turning up 2,000 revolutions per minute and only showing 65 on the air speed indicator. It was a desperate race to see whether we or the cloud would reach the pass first. Of one thing we were certain—there was not room for both the thunderstorm and ourselves in the pass. Only the thought of the miles of rough country behind kept us from turning back. I gave her the gun and opened up our Gipsy engine another 100 revolutions. We entered the pass. When we were almost through, it grew black; the cloud was upon us. To the left, however, over the shoulder of the mountain around which we had just come, we had caught a glimpse of a wide valley stretching off to the south. As we cleared the pass, we dove blindly over the shoulder on our left towards the valley. There was a dull roar. For a few seconds we were blinded by the rain and hail. We seemed to be flying in solid water as we dropped through the edge of the cloud. Flit was drenched and our faces were stinging, but on emerging from the cloud we saw below us rich green pastures affording an easy landing. It was a welcome sight made none the less so when behind us we saw gusts of heavy rain sweeping down the mountain and through the pass we had so recently vacated.

We maintained our altitude, cleared one more narrow range of peaks and looked down 8000 feet at the little city on the border of the Great Salt Lake. The Wasatch Mountains had been conquered! For a small plane Flit had stood up wonderfully under severe flying conditions. We throttled down the over worked motor and gave it a well earned rest and spent fifteen minutes gliding down across the city, over the spires of the Morman Temple to the landing field. It was only 12 o'clock but exhausted by the nervous strain of our last 350 miles, we felt we had had enough flying for the day.

We cleaned all the spark plugs, adjusted the valves and set the magneto points. Strangely enough, the leak in our main gas tank seemed to have disappeared. Could it have vibrated together or had it become clogged? In any case, there was no sign of a leak now, whereas the fabric on the trailing edge of the wing had been dripping with gasoline when we left Parco early the same morning.

That afternoon we realized that Salt Lake City was not as small nor was it as near the lake as our first glimpse that morning had led us to believe. We spent almost an hour motoring through the city and out to the lake, where we went in for a "float" on its salty waters.

IX

Wind and Wind Currents

OUR NEXT DESTINATION was Boise, Idaho. After sixty miles' flying over the streaky salt lake we had another pass of 9500 feet high to clear, but we were becoming used to mountains now. Also, we felt cheered for the mail pilots at Salt Lake had told us the passes we had come through from Parco were worse than any we should encounter between there and the coast. Within the past year two planes larger than ours had been turned over and lost in the tricky currents of that last pass.

Flying northwesterly along the high ridge of the Black Pine Mountains, we were headed for Burley, Idaho. To circumvent a very black, threatening cloud, we had just deserted a broad valley and cut across the shoulder of the ridge. Just as we were congratulating ourselves on escaping the cloud itself, we had our first experience with the terrific down-currents of air present on the outskirts of severe thunderstorms. It was raining fitfully. I was studying the map preparatory to landing at Burley when suddenly the plane seemed to go out from under me, and I found myself brought up with a jerk against the strap which held me in the cockpit. The motor coughed, fluttered and stopped. I pushed the stick forward quickly and put the plane into a dive to prevent losing flying speed. Before we knew what was happening, the altimeter showed a descent of over 500 feet, leaving us less than 1000 feet above the ground. As I eased the stick back, there was another violent jerk. The motor fluttered again and then took hold. During the sudden drop all the gasoline had gone to the top of the carburetor so that it could not flow into the motor and we were lucky the motor had not cut out entirely. If this could

27

happen at the mere edge of a thunderstorm, we were not interested in what thrills the center could produce.

The pilots at Salt Lake City had told us if we wanted gas at Burley to circle the town three times, as the manager of the airport also ran the garage and he would come out and give us gas. The black clouds behind us seemed to be gradually working up into the mountains, but the wind was squally and we did not care to waste any time in getting down. We made three short circles about 500 feet over the town and then landed. Out came an automobile with the garage man and gasoline.

We filled up with gasoline but he was out of oil. We would have taken on a little oil but decided we probably had enough to make Boise. We expressed concern at the weather but the manager of the field reassured us. He was a native of Idaho and knew the weather. "Those clouds are headed for the mountains. Burley will get neither wind nor rain out of them. If you wait a short time, even this little wind will disappear."

It was a very hot day and, while waiting for the storm to blow over, Pete and I accepted the garage man's invitation to ride to town and get some oil and ice cream soda. A man and a boy left at the field were to watch the plane. Not entirely satisfied with the weather, I kept looking back. The same cloud which we had so recently escaped seemed to be following our course instead of continuing into the mountains as predicted.

As I watched the cloud grow blacker and appear to draw closer. I thought of the unenviable predicament we should be in if the wind came up and blew Flit over while Pete and I were in town having an ice cream soda. A nice story we should have to tell to our friends at home! There was no hangar at the field in which to shelter the plane and if that cloud ever let go, neither two men nor four could hold Flit on the ground. At the next corner we turned and headed back to the airport. Already the wind was coming down the street in strong gusts, dust was flying and we felt a distinct foreboding of more wind to come. We tore along the rough road, over the railroad tracks, through the gap in the fence and on to the field! Even with a man on each wing Flit was showing signs of wanting to take to the air.

Our weather prophet admitted: "It looks more like that cloud is going to hit Burley than any all summer. Occasionally we do get a real thunderstorm, and then it blows pretty hard."

Pete and I held a hasty council of war. There was real wind in that cloud. It was coming toward us fast and if it really hit, we could not possibly keep Flit from turning over. Flit was safer in the air than on the ground!

The motor was still hot. The wind was coming down the runway, so we were right in position to take off. There was still time. I jumped into the cockpit, and Pete turned over the prop. The engine started on the first turn. Pete climbed in and we gave her the gun. With almost no run, Flit was lifted into the air in the most bumpy take-off of my experience. I pushed her nose down in order to gain speed and as soon as we had sufficient altitude, we banked sharply, reversed our course and sailed swiftly before the wind. It was like roaring down the back of a heavy following sea in a very small boat. We tore over the ground at 140 miles an hour and in fifteen minutes the storm clouds were well astern and we were once more enjoying comparatively smooth air, with sunlight on our wings. We had gone some miles north of our course but it did not take long to get back to the Snake River which was wriggling its course across the State of Idaho.

X

We Decide to Land

AWAY FROM THE STORM the atmosphere was very muggy and the temperature gauge on the motor continued to mount. I did not know how hot it might get without "freezing" but it was obviously in the danger zone. Knowing Flit was short of oil, we were afraid of burning out some bearings. The motor was still functioning perfectly but from our map we knew it was over forty miles to the nearest landing-field. Underneath, the country was far from smooth but there were some cultivated fields in which we might have put down. There was a good chance while so doing of breaking our undercarriage and tying ourselves up for a week or more, but we felt this involved small danger to ourselves. Between us and the next landing field were canyons and a rough river valley. If our motor froze over these, we should be out of luck. It was a hard decision to make but we decided we had better land. We headed for a large cultivated field, but as we neared the ground, the field turned out to be on a steep hillside. Landing here meant turning over. So we pulled Flit's nose up and climbed. The motor was getting hotter. A short distance ahead was a ranch house, the only one in the vicinity. Coming in low over this, we aimed for a small alfalfa field about 100 yards square. There was no wind to slow us up and after clearing a row of trees, the field was short. Slipping sharply until our wing almost touched the ground we just missed hitting a flock of turkeys. As we flattened out a few feet above the field, we frightened three horses into a wild run across country. Nearing the ground, we could see the field was no billiard table, so we "squashed in," tail first so that our tail skid would strike the ground first, slow us up and reduce the danger of nosing over in the rough field. It was not until our wheels struck and we felt a sharp bang, bang, bang, that we realized what was happening. The fields in that section are cut with furrows fully two feet deep running close together and used as irrigation ditches. We had come in across the furrows.

Pete and I jumped out to see what was left of the undercarriage. To our amazement it was still intact, and as cowboys and children came charging up on horseback from all corners of the field, Pete and I knelt and kissed the balloon tires which we had kept soft for just such an emergency and which had served us so well.

We were down safely at the town of Bliss, Idaho, but how to get off when our motor had cooled was another problem. Across the furrows was out of the question and with them was equally impossible, because they were so deep that with our wheels in the furrows, the propeller would strike the hills between.

A crowd of about thirty people had soon gathered from miles around, all wanting to touch the plane. They had seen us circling low and gliding down to earth and so came to see the crackup. It was the first plane they had ever seen at close range.

But our audience was helpful as well as curious. From the nearby farm we obtained a drag sled which we made fast under the tail skid. Then with the aid of a horse, half a dozen cowboys, and the encouraging remarks of the assembled multitude, we towed Flit down the furrows, across the end of the field, through the farm yard, and onto the main road.

Taking photographs on a trip like ours is one of the most difficult feats of the journey. At the time it seems like a terrific chore and hardly worth while. But in retrospect the photographs, and especially the moving pictures, are delightful reminders of countless experiences.

I do not know whether Pete had this in mind at the time but, with all the determination of a news photographer, he set to work recording by still and by movie cameras every detail of our forced visit. The assembled gathering were not unwilling to pose, although it seemed to me Pete spent an unnecessarily long time snapping three young ladies who had arrived on horseback. I was about to offer to help out, when I overheard the most alluring of Pete's three admirers ask if either of us were Lindbergh. Before I could say "Yes," Pete had admitted the truth. Perhaps it was just as well; with his one suit of clothes Pete could ill afford an attack of souvenir hunters.

We were not lacking in assistance. In addition to the horse attached to the tail skid there were three men on each wing and as many more supervisors. There was barely room for us to get Flit between the pigsty and the windmill. A flock of turkeys had to be "shooed" away from the side of the house and then we had to move the tubs beside the pump. Finally to the musical squeaking and grunting of several families of pigs, Flit was dragged slowly through the farmyard, with her wings scraping the house on the right and the fence on the left.

As we neared the highway, some new arrivals drove up in a Dodge, friends of the old farmer who was beside me helping with the wing.

"Whatcher doing?" inquired the new arrival with a good Idaho twang.

"Just some friends of mine come out from the East on business," replied the farmer.

"I'm glad we got that deal across," I interposed.

"So'm I. Yes, that ought to fix things all right. I've been wantin' that fer some time." Then turning to the new comer: "You wouldn't want a ride would you? Glad to have the boys take you up."

The road was wide enough and fairly smooth, although somewhat crowned. To take off to the eastward was out of the question. Here was an uphill grade and the single line of telegraph poles ran close to the fence which bordered the road. To the west was down a slight grade, but as the road swung gradually to the left the telegraph poles diverged a little to the right. This was our only chance, and with the wind still light from the westward it would give us a little help.

We left the plane at the side of the road while I motored back eight miles to the nearest town to get some oil. On my return a Union Pacific freight violated the state law by stopping on a crossing for more than eight minutes with the result that before we could finish putting oil in the motor, the wind had swung around and came in from the east. This meant a down wind take off, seldom desirable, and complicated in this case by the necessity of staying on a crowned surface while going around a gradual bend with a deep ditch to the left of the road and telegraph poles to the right.

I wondered as we said good-bye whether this was really farewell to Bliss or whether we might not be back in a few minutes to spend several more days attempting repairs on our plane.

A cowboy was sent ahead down the road to stop traffic. The motor roared, Flit wobbled slightly to the right, then to the left, then steadied. I remember Pete waved, prematurely, I thought. Then Flit felt lighter. We were off the ground; we were level with the telegraph wires, above them—now let him wave. Bliss, Idaho was only another incident in our trip west. I am sorry we have not a motion picture of that take-off. It would have been interesting to know how much we wobbled and how near we came to the ditches and fences on either side of the road.

XI

Joe

MOUNTAIN HOME was the next landing field—an emergency field of the Varney Lines, and only about 40 miles from Bliss. The sun was down, and it was already dusk as we flew low over the town and glided toward the field.

We tossed a coin and as tails won, I left Pete to tie down the plane for the night and started to walk the three miles to town to get an automobile. I was shuffling over the dusty road wondering why with all that open country airports were not built nearer town when the head-lights of an approaching automobile awoke me from my reverie. It was a Ford truck containing a man of foreign extraction and five of his offspring. The children had seen the plane fly over and insisted that it was going to land. Father was doubtful, but they demanded a ride to the field to make sure. I was grateful for the curiosity of the young.

In accordance with a decision made early in the trip, when we came to leave the field, I let Pete as a matter of course take the best seat beside the driver while I climbed in back. This decision had been forced upon us because of our mutual politeness. During the first couple of days of our trip it had become apparent that a great deal of time might be wasted in waiting for the other person to go first through doors; into cabs and at the hotel desks, it had always been "after you." At this rate we should have needed an extra week. Also, the question of paying and keeping accounts had become a daily complication.

We had finally hit upon the following happy solution. Both would contribute $25 to the pot. One man would carry the pot until it was all used up, and during this time he would make the arrangements, pay all expenses and would be entitled to go first on all occasions, while the other would bring up the rear with the parachute bag containing our traveling wardrobe. A desirable feature of this arrangement was that in order to prolong his superiority, the pot-bearer naturally economized wherever possible. Until we became accustomed to the arrangement there had been, to be sure, some public scenes where the luggage carrier was severely admonished but we quickly discovered there was always an opportunity for retaliation and soon became adapted to our social positions.

This time, having been relegated to the rear of the truck with the bag, I found compensation in the form of the five children. They were bright and clean and spoke very good English. On the way to town I learned that their parents were Basques and that twenty-eight years before, their father had come over from the Basque country in the Pyrenees, eighty miles behind Bilboa. Two-thirds of the people in Mountain Home were Basques. "Too many Basques," said one of the little boys. They had emigrated from the Pyrenees all the way to Idaho and settled down to their former occupation of sheepraising.

Of the two hotels in town, our driver recommended the Hotel Melon, for he was a friend of the manager's and knew it was clean and comfortable. Pete always had a way with these Westerners. By the time we had reached town he was calling the driver Joe, and as I dismounted with the bag, he tried to press a dollar into Joe's hand. Joe, however, staunchly refused, but he did very kindly agree to call for us at quarter of six the following morning to take us out to the field.

Pete signed the register while I with the bag stood at a respectful distance.

"Joe's quite a fellow," the hotel manager volunteered. We agreed.

"He's one of the biggest sheep herders around these parts. He just put $75,000 into a company down the line here a few weeks ago. He has a lot of interests around here."

After mounting to our room, I congratulated Pete upon his ability to judge his fellow men.

Joe was on hand at quarter of six sharp to take us to the field. He posed for his picture, but continued to decline Pete's less ardent offers of compensation.

Since it was Sunday morning, we had telephoned ahead to the manager of the airport at Boise to have someone at the field to "gas up" Flit. From Boise to Baker and over the Blue Mountains to Pendleton was more rough flying country but this time the mountains were covered with huge Oregon pines. We tried to decide in case our motor should quit whether to land the plane in the tree tops and with our "chutes" jump that long 200 feet to the ground or whether to jump with our parachutes immediately and trust to luck that the pines would not catch us as we dropped by and leave us dangling in midair.

A few days earlier the mail plane had come down in flames a short distance outside Baker. The pilot had been fortunate enough to escape with his life. Although we looked for the wreckage as we flew over, we saw no signs of it.

The air was comparatively bumpy over the mountains and continued so down the west side of the range to the lower "plains" around Pendleton. "Plains" they seemed at first, but on losing altitude we found that we were flying over rolling country and that the bare hills in contrast to the thickly wooded mountains had deceived us.

The field at Pendleton on the outskirts of the town was completely deserted when we landed. At one corner was a small shack, the door of which was padlocked; there were no other signs of gasoline.

About a quarter of a mile across the fields we spied a poor-looking frame house and on approaching found an Indian family gathered in the front yard. They were having lunch under a tree in an effort to keep cool. A sluggish-looking group they were, with their fat yellowish faces and dirty clothes. Whether it was from lack of desire or ability that they refrained from conversation with us, we did not know, but it was evident that they did not relish interruptions at their Sunday dinner. The best response we could get was a grunt from the elder male as he pointed over his shoulder toward the next house half a mile away and continued eating.

At this next farm house which was almost as dilapidated as that of the Indians we met a kindly old gentleman whose hospitable welcome made up for the indifference of the Indians. He offered us a refreshing drink of water from his pump. We thanked him very much.

"Oh, that's all right," he replied, "any time I can do anything, I'm glad to help. I'm an old fogey myself, but I believe in progress."

Turning away we met two cowboys coming in the driveway in a truck. They took us to town where we ordered gasoline, had lunch and got a road map as the best obtainable guide to Portland. The streets of Pendleton were hung with flags, the shop windows colorfully decorated and most of the men were wearing brilliant silk shirts. In three days the roundup, the greatest rodeo in the West, was opening and visitors and participants were already moving to town.

"By Wednesday the Indians will be pitching their tents in the main streets. For four days the town's wide open. Stay over and see the fun," they urged. "We'll take you in town and show you the roundup from the inside out."

It was a tempting offer, but we had a date with a bear in Alaska and no time to linger along the way, so were soon back at the dirtiest of flying fields. Above Pendleton the air was still bumpy and it became no smoother as we gained altitude and headed toward the Columbia River which wound down from the north before turning west to the Pacific.

XII

Columbia River Bumps

O F ALL THE EXCITING THRILLS we had on our trip
west I think our flight down the Columbia River gorge
on that bright Sunday afternoon stands foremost. I was
as frightened as at any time on the trip. The sky was
clear except for a few high scudding clouds and with
smooth air it would have been a glorious experience. The
Varney Air Mail pilots at Salt Lake City had told us the
Columbia River gorge was apt to be rough and they were
right. Red, the attractive young Irishman who had given
us such good advice, said he knew that country well. For
a long time there was a break in the Varney Air Mail line.
Planes did not fly from Pendleton to Portland on account
of the bad flying conditions. Then when they did open up
over this route a year or so ago Red was one of the first
pilots to fly it.

"You're apt to find the smoothest conditions about even
with the banks of the gorge," Red advised, "but if that's
bad, you might get down in the gorge. It's wide enough
so you can fly right down it."

Crossing the plains from Pendleton, we saw a number
of "wind twisters" with their dusty, spiral columns reaching
skyward several hundred feet and winding across the land-
scape. We did not like the appearance of these but kept
well above them and found that going over them simply
meant a slight bump. As we neared the river we dropped
down level with the banks which at this point were about
1500 feet above the river bottom.

Wind currents sweeping in from the steep hills and occasional mountains that rose precipitously on either side
of the river made the air very rough. It was difficult to

38

keep our light ship on even keel. We climbed to 6000 feet, but the winds whirled in from the higher mountains and made it just as rough. In desperation we dove into the gorge, lost all our hard-won altitude and flew along a few hundred feet above the river bed, only to learn this was no better. First we would be level with the banks, then the air would drop us down 200 feet inside the gorge, and the next minute an upcurrent would lift us 200 to 300 feet above the banks. The sun was still bright and the sky clear and could we have forgotten our predicament momentarily, the river gorge would have been a wonderful sight. But it was far from pleasure-flying; it was just a constant fight with the stick.

We marvelled that the wings stayed on. We were afraid to continue flying and equally afraid to land. Finally we decided to come down, if we could find a possible place, and wait for calmer weather. The river was widening ahead. We circled and came down on a small island that resembled a windswept sand dune at the edge of the river. On landing, we discovered Pete had a deep ridge in his right hand where he had been clutching the stick and mine had a large blister.

I was to cross the river to town and try to telephone ahead for a weather report. But before leaving Pete with Flit, it was necessary to tie down the wings. The wind was blowing so hard we were afraid to leave the plane unsecured with only one man.

A short distance up the river I was able to get a regular ferry boat which forded the fast waters on a wire cable to a town called The Dalles. Even the young ferryman commented on having seen us tossed around considerably as we circled over him before landing. During our conversation I asked him which was the best hotel in town.

"Well, that depends on how high class you are," he replied seriously.

At The Dalles I found the surface wind was blowing thirty-five miles an hour, and we had been bucking this wind. There was no way of telling how hard it was blowing up aloft where it swept between the mountains.

I telephoned ahead and found that there was a light

breeze at Portland, and at Hood River twenty miles below us the wind was blowing twenty miles an hour. Just below Hood River, the Weather Bureau warned us, was the famous Viento Point so named on account of its treacherous winds. Here the wind would be terrific on an afternoon like this, so we decided to leave Flit where she was for the night and fly in to Portland in the cool air of the following morning.

That evening while walking home to the hotel from the movies, our curiosity led us up to a large old fashioned barroom on the main street of The Dalles. From the sidewalk we could look back into the high-studded pool room, the walls of which were completely covered with animal heads. There must have been two hundred trophies.

Thus were we lured inside and as we stood there, each with one foot on the rail, sipping our drinks and feeling really western, the gentleman in riding clothes beside us insisted on showing us the muscles in his right arm. Since he was moderately intoxicated, we thought it better to take polite notice. It was an impressive sight. As he tightened his biceps, the muscles expanded and stood out in huge solid knots. Just then a friend strolled in. This gentleman was sober.

"That's nothing. Look at this," said the newcomer, rolling back his sleeve and disclosing an even more imposing array of muscular knots.

"How much do you weigh?" he queried of our first friend.

"One hundred and seventy," was the reply.

Whereupon the newcomer leaned down, placed the palm of his hand squarely on the other's seat. The intoxicated man leaned back, and the newcomer lifted him in a sitting posture on the palm of his hand and held him at arm's length above his head. It was a great display of brawn and muscle, but the altitude was too much for our intoxicated friend. He lost his balance and fell forward striking his forehead against the bar rail and giving himself a nasty cut above the eye. He was dazed for a minute and a little scared. We expected a fight, but not at all.

"Thar was a tough one—wasun' it?" he asked hopefully.

They were still friends when we left for our hotel.

XIII

Portland Through the Fog

F LIT HAD WEATHERED THE NIGHT successfully in
the beach grass, and we were in the air before seven
o'clock. Our decision in waiting over night was certainly
vindicated. There was a gentle breeze aloft, the sky was
clear and the air cool and smooth in contrast to the previous
evening. Gaining altitude and rising above the river banks,
we watched the sun's rays creep down the sparkling, snowy
face of Mt. Hood. As we cut over the mouth of the Hood
River where it entered the Columbia, we had a glorious view
up the river valley to the mountain itself. Although the banks
of the Columbia were getting lower and the gorge was less
pronounced, it was a picturesque flight all the way to Portland. It was only eighty miles and in less than an hour we
were nearing the city, which we found hidden under a blanket
of fog. The fog over the city and to the westward seemed to
be gradually dispersing in the sunlight, so we decided to
fly around for a little while and wait. Underneath us were
several golf courses. We flew low over these and tried to
pick places to land in case the fog should start to shut in. We
could see the early morning golfers gathered around the first
tee and the autos arriving at the club house. There were
several good fairways on which we might put down so we
were not at all disturbed, but as we flew around the fog did
not seem to be burning off in the slightest. I was anxious to
have a game of golf and thought of landing, playing the golf
right there on the course and flying into the airport later
when the fog burned off. But it was always less trouble to
land at an airport in the first instance, so we climbed to 3000
feet, about 1000 feet above the fog, and flew over the city
looking for a break through to the field. There was just a

41

blanket of soft white down underneath. We saw a plane coming over the fog from the north. She was below us and stood out sharply, her dark wings projected in the sunlight against a white fluffy background.

It gave one a weird sensation of living in another world— just two planes were flying around in the sunlight above the huge white billows of clouds. Only about half a mile below us and hidden from view was a large city living in the shade of a low fog, or heavily overcast sky. By the wing design and the radio bar, we recognized our companion plane as a mail carrier. After circling low over the clouds a few times the mail plane suddenly dove into a large white fluffy cloud and disappeared from view. She was some distance below us, and we estimated she could not have been more than 1500 feet above the ground when she entered the fog. It gave us quite a start to see her disappear but we decided the pilot must have known what he was doing; probably the airport was underneath. So we continued to circle in that neighborhood looking for a break through.

A short distance to the westward there was a small opening. We flew over and saw water and ships underneath. Then looking through at an angle, we saw grass and the yellow and black boundary markers of an airport. We came lower and on circling around could see there must be several hundred feet of ceiling underneath. Again we circled and, as the fog bank drifted slowly eastward, we lined up the hole at just the right angle and dove through in the direction of the airport. Underneath the fog there was a good 300-foot ceiling and fair visibility, but we did not even have to change our course as we glided into the smartest looking airport we had yet seen.

The field covered the whole of a large, oval-shaped island situated on a branch of the Columbia River due west of Portland. As we neared the ground, the field looked more like a park than an airport. Except for the runways, the entire island was covered with rich green grass and sprinklers played here and there all over the field. There were two cinder track runways running north and south with occasional cement cross channels connecting the two. One of the runways was marked in large letters for incoming planes and the other for outgoing. To the east of the runways and also stretching north and south was a row of half a dozen fine-looking hangars with a wide, smooth cement apron in front. The grass was in such beautiful condition that there was no necessity for having signs telling planes to keep off.

Pete's classmate, Lee Jameson, was in charge of the passenger department of the Boeing Airplane Company at Portland. Pete had written him of our trip, so we boldly taxied over to the main hangar of the Boeing System where all the mail and passenger ships report. Jameson was there and received us cordially, introducing us to officials, pilots and mechanics. Flit was immediately taken into custody by the mechanics and treated with the care of a Boeing trimotor. By the time we had registered, Flit had been oiled and cleaned. It gave us a feeling of comfort and pride to see trim, little Flit looking immaculate beside one of the big Boeing mail planes in a hangar which more resembled an automobile show room than any hangar we had seen.

It was 10 o'clock and Seattle was only 160 miles away. With the prevailing north wind this meant slightly over two hours of flying. We had been circling Portland for three-quarters of an hour waiting for a chance to land. We telephoned the Alaska Washington Airways Company at Seattle and found our pontoons had arrived the Saturday before and were being brought over from the freight yard that day. Mr. Goodwin, with whom we talked said they could start putting on the pontoons the following morning. What luck! Our schedule was working out perfectly; it seemed too good to be true.

With only two hours' flying ahead of us that day, we felt content and carefree. Pete stayed and had lunch with his friend, Lee Jameson; while I went out and played golf with the Boeing Operations Manager, Les Hubble. Les had been in the flying game for years and had been one of the first two pilots to run the flying boat service from Seattle to Victoria and Vancouver back in 1910. The original boat "Old Glory" had become a famous character on the coast.

"They had the old crate out and flew her last year," Les said. "You may see her at Seattle."

As it turned out, we did see her in the hangar at Lake

Washington. But there have been many changes in the last twenty years, and I would rather fly my Flit.

Les gave us some valuable suggestions about flying over the water. Incidentally, he said that although he had not been flying much of late, he had been up the day before but on account of the roughness stayed only ten minutes. It was one of the worst flying days they had had in Portland in a long time. Small wonder that we had found the Columbia River gorge too rough for comfort in little Flit.

Les also mentioned the mail plane we had seen landing through the fog and explained how such landings were accomplished. Quite often the Portland airport is shrouded by a veil of fog while all around is clear. Between Portland and the sea there is a range of low mountains in whose lee the fog settles, blanketing the nearby airport until the morning sun burns away the fog. Under these conditions the mail plane circles above the fog in the neighborhood of the field until the roar of its motor is heard on the field below. Then the radio operator at the field calls up and advises of conditions below. This morning the operator had called up by the radio telephones: "We have a 300-foot ceiling. We can hear you directly above us now. OK to come through."

True to form, Pete and I took so long seeing friends and playing golf that we had barely enough time to reach Seattle before dark. Nevertheless, we could not resist a brief meeting en route with another friend of Pete's working at Kelso. Fifteen minutes was a short time in which to renew a friendship after three years, especially when both men were fishermen. We promised to return for a weekend's fishing on our homeward journey, however. Now it was getting late and we still had 120 miles to go with a light head wind.

Heading north from Kelso we followed the Cowlitz River a few miles and flew directly over the edge of a large forest fire which was blazing furiously to the east of the river. Unused to such tremendous forest fires, we were distressed to see the huge firs and pines wreathed in flames with no possible check in view until the autumn rains. As we neared Tacoma, more smoke drifted in from other fires on the Olympic Peninsula to the west and the atmosphere became so thick we were forced down to less than 1000 feet in order not to lose sight of the ground. As there were many hills from two to three thousand feet high in the vicinity, we went out over Puget Sound in order to avoid the risk of crashing into one of them in the smoke. At Tacoma, we headed inland following the railroad tracks to Renton Field on the shore of Lake Washington, Seattle.

Jump Goodwin, field superintendent of the Alaska Washington Airways Company was on hand to greet us as we landed and by the hangar stood an attractive couple waiting for Pete.

"Is this the first time a Dartmouth man ever went West?" I asked a little sourly, as Pete hurried over to greet his friends, Don and Marcella McDermott. But this time they were not Dartmouth friends who were insisting we come and stay with them; perhaps it was something in Pete's personality after all.

XIV

Alaska Washington Airways
Is Good to Us

A T THE OFFICE of the Alaska Washington Airways Company, Commander Eckmann, the Chief Pilot, generously spent an hour with me going over our charts from Seattle to Skagway. He pointed out the salmon canneries where we could get gasoline and the settlements where there were floats or slips at which we could tie up Flit for the night. He gave us letters to all their northern officials and asked us to report to their offices each night whenever possible so they might know of our whereabouts in case we met with difficulties or got lost.

The president of the company, Mr. J. L. Carman, Jr., was a friend of our host's. Since writing me, he had had a change of heart about the wisdom of our flying north in such a little ship. No small plane had ever made the trip to Alaska and there were long and lonesome hops. As further encouragement we recalled the farewell remarks of my friend, Ernie Swigert, at Portland: "If you don't crack up, those Kodiak bear will get you."

"Ernie was a war pilot and has hunted bear in Alaska, so he ought to know," we reflected.

At the field Jump Goodwin took charge of preparing Flit for the trip north. The motor was checked, the valves adjusted, the magneto points cleaned and the oil changed. The main gas tank had opened up again on the way from Salt Lake City, so that the wing fabric had to be removed and the tank soldered. The wheels were exchanged for pontoons; pneumatic life vests, a deflatable rubber boat and paddles were substituted for parachutes.

46

The morning of our departure from Seattle we received a telephone call from our friends in the Boeing Company at Portland. They were disturbed about the possibilities of our getting through British Columbia without a Federal registration or a Federal pilot's license. By saying a good word for us to the Department of Commerce Inspector in Seattle, they had hoped to assist in getting the necessary Federal licenses. But the Seattle inspector was out of town for two days, and as my eyes had never passed the tests in Boston, I could not see how they would be improved much by the atmospheric conditions around Seattle. We could not wait two days for a license we might not get and as far as the United States was concerned a Federal license was not necessary for us to engage in interstate or foreign commerce. Once we were out of the State of Washington, British Columbia was our only hurdle. A non-stop flight of a thousand miles would do it, but unfortunately our maximum cruising radius with both tanks and no wind was four hundred miles. Here we would have the prevailing winds to buck.

It has always been my theory that most officials are reasonable if treated reasonably. We did have an identification certificate from the Department of Commerce which might pass as a registration in a pinch. Moreover, what would a customs officer in a small British Columbia town know about United States private aeroplane licenses? So we asked Commander Eckmann to name the smallest port on the coast of British Columbia which had a customs collector, and the Commander gave us a letter of introduction to "The Honorable Collector of Customs, Alert Bay, B. C."

By Wednesday noon we were ready to start, that is, if Flit could get off the water with our increased load. The pontoons weighed an extra hundred pounds, and we had the Springfield rifle Pete had shipped west with enough cartridges to start a world war. We were leaving behind our so-called respectable clothes and had discarded shoes in favor of sneakers, but in addition to the deflatable rubber boat and paddles, Jump Goodwin had insisted upon our taking a whistle, bell, fog horn, flares, anchor, line and other seagoing equipment, including a copy of the pilot rules to qualify us as an ocean-going vessel while taxiing on the water. As running lights were the accessories we lacked, we promised Jump we would beach Flit every night before dark. It was just as well Flit did not have a Federal registration, as the Department of Commerce would never have approved our setting out with such a load.

The usual morning smoke and fog were still hanging low over Lake Washington when I took Flit up for the test hop. The speed with which she climbed on to the step of the pontoon and then took to the air was quite astonishing. In no time she was up a thousand feet and the shore line was barely visible through the smoke. When I taxied back to the float, I found Jump thrilled with Flit's performance. He said we need not worry about overloading that plane; we could take along a couple of passengers. He had never seen a pontoon job leave the water more easily. As Jump was an old Navy mechanic, now in charge of the Alaska Washington fleet of Lockhead Vegas on pontoons, I took his remarks with a grain of salt, but Flit's behavior on pontoons was at all times a pleasant surprise.

"At what speed do you usually run your motor?" Jump inquired.

"Anywhere from 1800 to 1900 revolutions."

"When you are making long hops, change your revolutions every half hour or so," he suggested. "If you have been running at 1800 throttle her down till she stops vibrating and then open up to 1850 or 1900. It will change the vibration period and save your ship. Also, your gas tank won't open up so quickly. I try to get our pilots to do it but they don't like to because it's so much easier to set the throttle and let her go until they get there."

This was a new thought for us and a very logical one—another little pointer for cross-country flying of which we had received so many to date.

XV

We Start North

IT WAS AFTER 1:30 BEFORE THE smoke had cleared sufficiently for us to venture up the shore of Lake Washington over the ship canal through the heart of Seattle to Puget Sound. Although some smoke stayed with us for the better part of a hundred miles, conditions improved after we had cleared the Olympic Peninsula. As we made our way up the sound between Vancouver Island and the mainland, we could see the forest fires burning in the distance along the west coast of the island.

We soon discovered that cruising on pontoons along the inland passage and flying low over strange waters and strange islands is infinitely more fun than flying overland at high altitudes. As we went farther north and the atmosphere cleared, the day turned out to be bright and sunny and the flight up the coast was fascinating. At times, when following the navigation aids of the steamship passage, we were only two or three hundred feet above the water; then as the steamship lane wound around the islands, we would rise and hop over two or three islands, occasionally dodging between mountains which rose to five or six thousand feet. Usually we were within gliding distance of the ocean or some pretty inland lake. The towns and other signs of civilization were rapidly thinning out and we checked the occasional fishing canneries on the chart as ports of refuge in case we had to put down. Believing it wise to have friends in our neighborhood, we often zoomed low over the numerous fishing boats and gave them a friendly wave. The crews were always ready to respond.

Confronted with our Federal license and customs problems, we had chosen Alert Bay as a rather ambitious destination for that first afternoon. Accordingly, we had taken off with a full load of gas in both tanks. Before we had covered a quarter of our 400-mile hop, Pete reported another leak, however, in the lower gasoline tank. The seam had opened and again there was a steady drip between his feet. As fast as we used up the gas in the upper tank, we pumped the contents of the lower tank into it. It was a nuisance to have this occur just when we were leaving civilization and wanted to refuel with all the gasoline we could carry. The lower tank was soon dry, however, and we were able to forget this worry and devote our entire attention to the beautiful and rapidly changing panorama of the inland passage.

We exchanged occasional superlatives through the voice tubes and the time passed so quickly and so pleasantly that before we realized it, we were gliding over the picturesque little fishing village of Alert Bay. The sun was just setting behind the opposite hill as we slipped down on to the glassy surface for our first landing within British Columbia. We had been in the air for five and a half hours, our longest non-stop flight. As I climbed out of the cramped quarters, my respect increased considerably for the solitary ocean fliers who sit for thirty odd hours in similarly confined positions.

Alert Bay is located on the inner curve of a crescent-shaped island. Possibly the town stretches for two miles along the rocky beach, but at no place does it reach more than a couple of hundred yards inland from the shore. The one street consisted of a dirt road or path extending the length of the town and following closely the curve of the beach. The houses were a mixture of log cabins and frame buildings, painted and unpainted.

We taxied in to the Imperial Oil Company dock where the manager stood beckoning us away from the dock of the Union Oil Company opposite. We postponed refueling until the morning and the manager, anxious to help us in every way possible, showed us to a mooring where we secured Flit for the night. As we turned to row to the beach, a heavy fog rolled in rapidly over our stern, and the sturdy little auxiliary fishing boats which a minute before had been plainly visible around the point were lost to view, although

Northern Scenes: Beautiful Mole Harbor, Admiralty Island

The Fishing Fleet at Anchor in Alert Bay, British Columbia

An Indian Graveyard, With Totem Poles, Also at Alert Bay

Not All Our Friends Were Harvard or Dartmouth. On the left, Mrs. McDermott, of Seattle, and on the right an Idaho Miss.

still audible as they chugged in to the harbor through the darkness.

These fogs were typical of the coast, and we were lucky to have landed just when we did. A half-hour later, and we should have been forced down to shift for the night on the shore of some uninhabited island. But we were prepared for such emergencies and with a landing field always at hand we had little to worry us, so long as our motor functioned.

The fishing village of Alert Bay boasts a possible five hundred inhabitants, the great majority of whom are Indians. Picture our surprise upon calling at the house of Mr. Potts, the Collector of Customs, to be told by the young lady who opened the door that her father was out at a bridge party and to call the following morning.

We did call the following morning, and were received by Mr. Potts with lukewarm cordiality. Upon learning that we tried to report to him immediately upon arrival, his attitude warmed perceptibly. He inquired for our Federal N. C. number or Federal Registration number. We assured him this was not necessary for private flying in the United States. The letter from Commander Eckmann did the rest and from then on we were the best of friends. Mr. Potts told us how the winter before Commander Eckmann had flown to an inland lake near Juneau to rescue a woman who was suffering from appendicitis. By brilliant flying in the face of adverse conditions, he had carried her to a hospital in Vancouver in time to save her life and the coastal residents of British Columbia and Alaska were not likely to forget his deed.

Seaplanes were not infrequent visitors at Alert Bay, but the diminutive size of Flit created quite a stir among the fishing population. She looked too small to fly. In spite of her size I was required to make out a regular ship's manifest to enter Flit in British Columbia, reporting a cargo of "Ballast and Stores," and signing "L. M. Lombard, Master." As I walked out of Mr. Potts' office proudly folding the Canadian clearance papers in my pocket I, too, began to feel impressed with the importance of our expedition.

Although the Indian cemeteries here, guarded by thunder birds, huge serpents and other weird totem poles, are said to be among the best in existence, Alert Bay is still quite unspoiled by tourists. A number of the largest totem poles raise their ugly figures right on the main street in the center of the town. Prayers are offered to the thunder birds when rain is needed and we were told that each of the various poles had its own particular significance.

Before starting on our trip, pessimistic friends in the east had warned us of the scarcity and expense of gasoline in Alaska. The next morning when we paid 25 cents a gallon for aviation gas which cost us 30 cents in Boston, we had our first pleasant surprise on this score. To be sure this was not Alaska, but we were moving north.

The fog hung low at the entrance of Alert Bay all the forenoon, and again it was not until after luncheon that we got underway. Even this delay was not without its compensations. The evening of our arrival we had had dinner at the Alert Cafe. As we sat upon the stools before the counter, the swinging door opened, and the bright enigmatic countenance of a Chinaman appeared. His wide pop eyes opened even wider as he stared at us. Suddenly he burst forth with a merry "Ha-ha ha, ha, ha, —ha, ha—you Amelican? Ha, ha, —you come in eloplane?" and before we could reply, he continued with his contagious, but unaccountable chuckles. Although not entirely flattered, Pete and I were soon helplessly ha, ha-ing back at him. We ordered dinner and he returned with food, never what we ordered; but as he put it before us with his infectious ha-ha, ha, there was little we could do. So the next noon we were glad to return in a vain effort to discover the cause of "Ha Ha's" hysteria.

XVI

The Fascinating Inland Passage

T HE TRIP from Alert Bay to Prince Rupert unfolded another fantastic panorama of thickly forested, mountainous islands and high inland lakes, winding waterways, and precipitous wooded fiords. As we got further north, snow capped mountains appeared on the horizon to the north and east. It was much like the scenery of the preceding day, but more fascinating, more unusual. At times we climbed to three or four thousand feet, looked over the islands and headlands and studied the map spreading out before us. The infinitely varied shapes of the islands made navigation easy and amusing. It hardly seemed like navigating in strange waters, for with such a variety of landmarks with which to check the dead reckoning, it was impossible to lose one's way on a clear day.

To reduce the danger from dripping gasoline we had put only five gallons in the forward tank and pumped this into the upper tank as soon as there was room. This shortened our cruising radius, and a fresh north wind necessitated our landing at the little settlement at Swanson Bay for refueling.

Swanson Bay was formerly the home of a large lumber and pulp mill. Some of the surrounding hills were still bare as a result of the wholesale cutting. Cheaper timber further south had put the mill out of business so that now there remained only a deserted village with a small headquarters for fishing boats. The Imperial Oil Company had a seaplane base there so we found a perfect slip for landing and refueling.

While approaching Swanson Bay, we had had a fair wind between the islands. Abreast of the semicircular bay there was a calm spot. A short distance north a clear line of ruffled water warned us we should soon be buffeted by the cool fresh north wind again. These conditions were not infrequent when flying among the islands. The winds would sweep in opposite directions around the steep mountains or around the opposite ends of the islands. On occasions we saw little fishing boats sailing in the same direction on opposite tacks within a comparatively short distance of one another, each heeled well over under a good fresh breeze. Sailing up the inland passage on a breezy day was fraught with thrills and disappointments as the fluky winds headed or favored in rapid succession.

As Flit entered the air above the ruffled water north of Swanson Bay, she bucked a little and slowed down, just as a speed boat on the surface below would have bucked on entering the rough water. To complete the simile, I felt a dash of spray in the face but strangely enough this spray carried with it a strong odor of gasoline. Had the upper tank opened up again? Looking aloft, I saw a steady spray of gasoline blowing back over my head, apparently from the top of the tank. This was serious, so I told Pete to take the controls. I loosened my belt and by climbing up in the seat, I could see the top of the tank. The cover of the tank was flapping in the breeze, and the gas was bouncing out of the full tank and blowing away to leeward. After refueling at Swanson Bay, we had neglected to put the cover on the tank and had not noticed it until striking the rough air. The little chain had saved the cap from going overboard. Thinking of the endurance fliers who walk all around their planes on catwalks to oil, refuel, and make minor repairs, I tried to climb up in the cockpit high enough to reach the gas cap. It was not far to reach, but the wind was terrific and the hand holds only fair. Without a parachute the water looked a long distance below. So we glided back to land on smooth water to remedy our carelessness.

Again it was a glassy surface where we landed at Prince Rupert that evening. The sun had set, the sky was a myriad of colors, and the long mysterious reflections from the mountains and trees made landing very deceptive. We came in close to the row of wharves so as not to misjudge the water. A snug little berth behind the Imperial Oil dock afforded

Flit complete shelter for the night and we were assisted in tieing her up by Harry, a young Canadian who had flown "D. H.'s" in the R. A. F. during the war but who had not been up since. It seemed good to be fooling around a plane again, he said.

In spite of a gorgeous sunset, we awoke the following morning to find a heavy rain and thick fog. The morning was spent entering Flit with Mr. McLeod, the very hospitable Collector of Customs, getting clearance papers for Alaska, refueling and discussing the weather with the fishing captains. Anxious to be on our way if possible, we radioed Ketchikan, our next refueling point, less than 150 miles away, for a weather report. "Three to four thousand foot ceiling and visibility about ten miles," was the answer. If we could only get through! Here we were within two hours' flight of Alaska, our destination, and hopelessly fogbound. The government wireless station was located on Digby Island, across the entrance to Prince Rupert Harbor, about ten miles distant. Some of the fishermen thought it might be clear beyond the island, but as there was not any wind, the consensus of opinion was that it would probably be worse outside. We telephoned over to Digby, and they reported fog as thick as soup.

We finally accepted our fate, borrowed a rowboat from our friend Harry at the oil dock, and rowed across the bay for some fishing at the mouth of the McClintock River.

XVII

A Fisherman's Paradise

I HAD NEVER CONSIDERED myself an Izaak Walton with the rod. In the days of my youth I had been known to sit for hours in an open boat under a blazing sun and flick a fly about without the slightest suggestion of a rise. Also a number of hours of my life had been devoted to untangling very tenacious hooks from the even more tenacious foliage guarding our New England streams. I once caught a brook trout in the Canadian Rockies. I can boast of having an Irish lake trout to my credit and numerous salt water trophies from puffing pigs to sharks, but I cannot say that I am an ardent fisherman. Pete, on the other hand, had brought two rods, a couple of reels and hundreds of elaborate hooks— out of all proportion to the amount of luggage our limited space permitted.

It may make the picture more convincing, to tell how as we rounded the point and reached our fishing ground, Pete almost upset the boat from pure excitement. On all sides there were fish jumping—salmon two and three feet long. The jumping was continuous, not simply one at a time, but several fish were often in the air simultaneously. It was beyond all belief—just a fisherman's dream.

We approached cautiously to photograph the jumping salmon with both the still and motion picture cameras but our caution was unnecessary. There were so many fish we could not frighten them and we were able to get some quite unusual close-ups of jumping salmon as evidence for un-believing friends. These were mostly humpbacked salmon, apparently having their last fling before going upstream to spawn and die. We soon discovered they were not in a rising mood, so we put a heavy jig hook on the line, cast, let it settle, then jerked the rod. Two out of three times we had jigged a good sized salmon.

According to a fisherman's standards this is not real fishing. It would never do for the truth to get home to our fishing friends so we planned to take photographs of the casting and landing. If we fouled the poor fish too far from its head, we made the hook fast to its mouth, threw it back into the water and landed it all over again for photographic purposes. This process seemed too cruel to repeat more than a couple of times and cutting the films to deceive the audience was so much trouble we have finally decided to publish the truth.

That evening I wrote in our Scientific Notebook: "The humpback salmon were not rising at the mouth of the McClintock River on the afternoon of August 29, 1930, but a number of fish did jump out of the water." Scientists must be moderate in their statements.

For a while it was great fun casting and playing the salmon. It became monotonous, however, as it was far too easy. All the fish had to be thrown back, for we had no use for them. This seemed cruel even though we knew that they were all doomed to die when they went upstream and spawned. In my opinion this is always the trouble with fishing, either you sit for hours without catching anything, which is not much fun, or the fish are so thick the sport soon becomes monotonous and loses its sporting elements. Or to put it another way, Pete was the fisherman of the expedition.

Toward dusk Harry and three friends came along in an outboard motor boat and asked us to join them at Harry's camp for supper. Of our catch, we had saved two for supper, but not until we produced these at camp were we informed that salmon fishing was out of season. It was too late now, and we ate them with relish. Harry's camp was on the shore of a cove across the bay from Prince Rupert. After supper our hosts entertained us with their orchestra, composed of an accordion, banjo, mandolin and drum. With very little urging, we accepted their invitation to spend the night.

The next morning it was still thick.

"Yer can't never tell. It may burn off by noon, or it may

last all day." This was too much! It was exasperating. Here we were within 100 miles of the Alaskan border idling away our time. We could not just sit here indefinitely!

The halibut fisherman Clipper II was leaving in about half an hour bound north. Her speed was eight knots. After getting out of the winding channel beyond Digby Island her captain was going to put out to sea, but he said he would be glad to lead us through the channel which would at least start us on our way. So we said farewell to Harry and his friends and cast off.

"Yes, Harry, I know we promised to stop on the way home and you assured us another party with the salmon, the orchestra and the drums. But with a strong tail breeze on the homeward voyage we shot by Prince Rupert at better than 100 miles an hour. Prince Rupert was still hidden under the heavy morning fog bank, and you couldn't have expected us to stop. But we shall try to come again."

Flit started on the first turn as usual, in spite of two nights and a day sitting in the fog and rain. We taxied slowly through the fog in the wake of Clipper II. It was amusing to taxi along on the surface of the smooth water in the wake of an Alaskan fishing boat. The channel was narrow and winding inside Digby Island, and as the fog was thick, we followed our lead closely.

A few miles outside the harbor entrance, the fog lifted. As Clipper II was bound to the west of our course, we thanked the skipper and took to the air, setting our course straight for Duke Point across sixty miles of practically open water. After a few minutes we saw another bank of fog ahead, drifting slowly in from the sea. We rose to look over this bank, but seeing no break, slipped sharply to reach the water again before the fog should separate us from our landing field. By this time we were well out to sea and taxiing through a fog so thick that at times we could hardly see the wing tips gave us an uncanny feeling. While flying, one loses one's perspective of distance. Thirty miles is nothing in a plane, whereas a thirty-mile sail in a small boat from Cape Cod to Nantucket always seemed like quite an adventure to me. The recollection of this was not very reassuring; neither was the sudden realization that we were at least fifteen miles from the nearest land, afloat on pontoons much less seaworthy than any sail boat. But in a heavy fog, there is small likelihood of wind and the water was smooth. As we could almost feel the sun burning through the haze, we decided to continue slowly on our way, with Pete in the front cockpit blowing our fog horn at regular intervals as though we were some great ocean liner. In spots the fog was lighter and we would speed up to twenty or thirty knots, depending on the visibility. Within an hour the fog had burned away sufficiently for us to venture aloft and, as there seemed to be a general breaking up of the fog bank, by flying over a few remaining clouds, we were able to land at Ketchikan about noon.

XVIII

Alaska Welcomes Us

AT LAST WE HAD FLOWN to Alaska! As if in response to our inward feelings of accomplishment, we received the warmest welcome to date. Ours was the first small plane to fly to Alaska, we were told.

Except for a brass band, we could not have asked for a more enthusiastic reception. The United States Customs officer and the newspaper reporter almost came to blows in their desire to be the first to interview us. As soon as we announced we were simply on a pleasure trip and had come to Alaska to hunt bear, the whole town wanted to advise us where to go. I left Pete to give a good story to the reporter while I walked up to the office with the Collector of Customs and made my apologies for not having telegraphed him of our approach.

How could I have telegraphed? How did we know when we could get through the fog? Our oversight was strictly against regulations and could have been considered a serious slight to the United States. Like entering ships we were supposed to wire our prospective time of arrival and the normal fine for not doing so was $500. Finally in our case, however, the United States decided to overlook our negligence. We turned in our Canadian clearance papers, and I signed another manifest to the effect that U. S. Seaplane Flit numbered M 137, with a cargo of ballast and stores and a crew of one in addition to the master, had just arrived from Prince Rupert, B. C. en route from Boston, Mass., to Juneau, Alaska, L. M. Lombard, Master.

We might never return to tell our doubting friends in Boston, but at least the records would prove that we officially reached our extreme destination.

Now the only question was where to go to hunt bear. There was the Stikine River Valley which had been recommended before we left Boston. That was good country, the Collector said, but it was in British Columbia and that would mean a two days' boat trip up the river from Wrangel. The river was too rapid for landing a plane.

On our returning to the float, the Collector introduced me to one gunner after another and they all offered good suggestions. There was Mr. Thacher of the gun store. He suggested one of the islands off Juneau, Admiralty Island, for example, where there were big bear. If we saw any, they were sure to be big ones, he assured us, since only the Alaskan brown or Kodiak bear live on that island. This was interesting, as we had heard of the Alaskan brown bear as the largest in existence.

Another gunner assured us there were plenty of bear in the woods right up in back of the town—black bear to be sure, but good sized ones.

"I wouldn't put foot on one of those islands for money," I overheard one man remark, "Those brown bear are man-eaters and bullets don't stop 'em."

"Oh, a man's safe enough if he's a good shot," another interposed.

Again I thought of the ducks I had missed at Eastham. Fearful lest they might ask me what kind of a gun I carried (I had forgotten the size of Pete's) or how many bear I had shot, I edged behind Pete and let him do the talking.

The consensus of opinion was that we should talk with the game warden, an excellent shot. He would know the best place for us to go. We were ushered into one of the rare automobiles which graced the town and driven to the end of the main street. The game warden was in and glad to talk to us. He was a big, rawboned, kindly looking individual of about forty, yet appeared as hard as nails. I had an immediate feeling of sorrow that he was not going to accompany us in search of bear. With him along I might not have to be such a good shot.

"You mustn't miss the chance to go off to the islands," he assured us after we had told him our problem. "There's no way of getting in touch with old Hasselbourg, but you might get a guide named Close who was up there last season."

Close lived a little further out of town and the warden took us out to talk with him. Sure, Close could go, but he thought the best place was Freshwater Bay on Chichogoff Island, just outside Admiralty, for he had noticed tracks when there last spring. However, Freshwater Bay was 250 miles airline over islands and open water, and this meant flying up with Close, leaving him on the island and coming back for Pete—three trips each way or 1500 miles in all.

"Why not try this fellow 'Old Hasselbourg' you all talk about?" we asked. "We've been lucky so far. We might be again."

We opened our chart and they pointed out a little bay at the southern end of Admiralty Island on the west shore of the Seymour Canal. They told us Hasselbourg used to have a camp on the creek at the head of that bay. Rather meagre, this description of an inlet 250 miles away, we thought.

"It's a beautiful harbor. You can't miss it," they said encouragingly.

That settled it. We hurried back to Thacher's, got two Alaskan game licenses, and by 3:30 that same afternoon we were on our way to Mole Harbor, Admiralty Island, in search of "Old Hasselbourg."

XIX

Old Hasselbourg

As WE GAINED ALTITUDE outside Ketchikan, we could look over Gravina Island and see the fog still lying thick toward the west. Nearing Wrangel, we searched in vain for the regular steamship lane up the inland passage, but even this was submerged in fog. We flew above it for awhile, then up a fiord, through a mountain pass, and behind the next range of mountains where we found narrow inlets and frequent inland lakes as our only landing fields. But here the weather was bright, the air smooth, and we were able to tear off the miles. The only danger was that if we had had to put down, we should have been miles from the steamship lanes or any habitation, or had we landed in an inland lake behind a mountain we might have been weeks getting out. At times the fiords were confusing in their similarity and once we went for some distance up the wrong one before discovering our mistake.

The snow-covered mountains behind Wrangel made a beautiful background for the city as we flew past, while in the foreground the white inverted images of these same mountains were reflected upon the pale green surface of the waters before the city. From our altitude the waters below the surface seemed stirred to a thick green by the glacier streams flowing down from the snowy background.

As we flew north the distances became more deceptive in the clear luminous air. Ice-capped mountains and glaciers to the east, which according to the charts were thirty or forty miles distant, seemed right beside us. One wooded peak which rose before us across a thirty-mile expanse of glassy water seemed almost within gliding distance.

In three hours we rounded a headland and from our chart

we knew our destination was at hand. What a beautiful harbor it was! By circling over it, we located the creek. Although an old dilapidated boat was rotting on the bank, we saw no camp nor other signs of life and feared the place had been deserted. Several large flocks of ducks took to the air as we landed and taxied in to the beach. Pete started up the creek to look for Hasselbourg, while I stayed to keep Flit afloat. Had we left the plane for half an hour she would have been marooned on the beach as the tide was ebbing and the chart showed a twenty-foot rise and fall at this point.

Pete had scorned my suggestion that he take a gun on this bear-infested island so, after a few restless minutes, I climbed the bank to make sure he was safe. There, about 100 yards away, was Pete engaging in a conversation with Robinson Crusoe himself. I shall never forget my first picture of the man. All I could see appearing through the reeds was a white face above a long, bushy beard. I ran to join them and was introduced to Mr. Hasselbourg. Here was a primitive man indeed. Pete was just explaining that we had heard he was the best guide in Alaska.

"Well, if you want some bear, you ought to be able to get them," our friend drawled out. "There are plenty of them around. You ought to have been here yesterday. There were two of them right about where your plane is. Big fellows they were, too."

It seemed too good to be true. We were at Mole Harbor and this was Hasselbourg. He had planned to go over to the mainland early the next morning after mountain goat with his fifteen-year-old nephew, Raymond Sheppard, who had come from Florida to spend the summer with him. Since we could only hunt for a few days, he guessed he could put that off.

"Your plane will be high and dry in a few minutes. Bring her up the creek alongside my boat where she'll be afloat at all tides."

So we followed Hasselbourg up the channel and moored Flit on a bridle less than a quarter of a mile from his cabin. We covered the engine and cockpits, and carried our scant luggage up the path.

"The Game Commissioner at Ketchikan told us if you

were absent, he thought you wouldn't mind our breaking in to spend the night," we said as we approached the door.

"It would have been all right today, but usually I leave a set behind the door to keep the Indians from breaking in during the fishing season."

That was interesting. "What is a set?"

"Oh, that's just a sawed-off shotgun with three or four slugs of powder in it and a five-inch bolt rammed down the muzzle. It ought to get you about amidships if you tried to open the door."

I made a mental note to so inform the warden in case he might, in the future wish to revise his directions to Mr. Hasselbourg's estate.

The cabin, a small, shingled, one-room affair with an attic above, was flanked on one side by a long shed. A door in the end wall of the shed formed the entrance to the cabin. This entire wall was a door suspended by hinges from the roof, and could be opened inwards by means of a pulley attachment to the ceiling. It was behind this wall that he placed the "set." Neatly arranged at the end of the shed were the rudimentary tools and equipment essential to a simple, self-supporting existence. There were carpentry tools, farm implements and above the bench which stretched the length of the shed were hung heavy leather boots, rubber boots and a few pieces of warm clothing. A smaller door led from the shed to the one room of the cabin itself. In the obscure light from the window we could see the unpainted plank walls, and the well-scrubbed floor. The furniture consisted of a small wood stove, one table, three chairs and a bench or couch built in the wall. In one corner was a small shelf holding guns, amunition and a wash basin, and above the couch another shelf containing books on animals, bird life and flowers and a few on Alaskan history and Arctic expeditions. A small, solitary window overlooking the creek and marshes to the East could be heavily boarded from within to keep out curious bears. The walls were bare except for three charts of the Alaskan coast. The whole atmosphere of the cabin was of simplicity to the point of frugality. This was not the place for comforts; only essentials mattered.

As soon as we entered the cabin, Hasselbourg started
the fire and my brief survey of surroundings was interrupted
by a strong smell of venison.

"The kid shot this buck the other day; we'll have to get
another if you're going to stay."

This sounded simple enough and not at all unpleasant.

In the cabin, Hasselbourg's demeanor was of a serious
vein, in keeping with the surroundings. Our well-intentioned
offers of assistance were declined. He built the fire, cooked,
and when dinner was over, washed and wiped the dishes
in a mechanical, efficient manner with no waste of time or
effort. We noticed this in his conduct throughout our visit.
He was so used to waiting on himself any interruption to
his course of habit, helpful though it seemed to us, an-
noyed, rather than pleased him. We confined ourselves to
fetching water from the spring and occasionally sweeping
out the cabin. He preferred to do unassisted the domestic
tasks affecting the cuisine. After the first day, I was usually so weary that this arrangement was entirely satisfactory
to me.

XX

Admiralty Island

ADMIRALTY ISLAND (always pronounced Admiral-ity by those of us who have been to Alaska) lies about twenty-five miles off the coast, west and a little south of Juneau, the capital of the Territory. One hundred miles long and forty miles across at its widest point, it extends north and south paralleling the coast line of southeastern Alaska. Along its eastern side, stretching south for sixty miles from almost the northernmost end of the island, is a long, narrow peninsula separated from the main body of the island by a broad inlet called the Seymour Canal. Mole Harbor breaks into the western shore of the Seymour Canal about opposite the end of the peninsula.

Except for three fish canneries operating on the west coast during the summer months, Hasselbourg is the only inhabitant of the island. His homestead of 160 acres is patented at Washington and the rest of the island is part of the Great Alaskan forest reserve. In front of Hasselbourg's cabin is a large area of cleared land, cleared partly by himself and partly by his predecessors. Except for a few inland lakes and some open meadows or "parks," as he called them, in the uplands, the island is heavily forested. In places, the luxuriant growth of timber, bushes and small plants is so thick as to constitute a veritable jungle. There are a number of mountains on the island over 4000 feet high, the highest being 4626.

During our visit we learned a little of the history of Admiralty Island. In years gone by, there had been an Indian settlement on the cleared knoll abreast of which Flit was now moored. On this knoll, Hasselbourg had planted a large part of his garden and there discovered many

Indian relics which he had donated to the museum at Juneau and which now formed the major part of the Indian Collection. About 1880, it seems, the Indians near Wrangel acquired firearms, before any other Indians in the neighborhood. To practice with their weapons they came to Admiralty in their long wooden boats and proceeded to exterminate the Indian tribe which was already located there.

About 1890, before the reign of Hasselbourg upon the island, his predecessor, a white trapper, had built a cabin on the very spot where Hasselbourg's now stood.

"The bears finally got him," Hasselbourg said briefly.

Our first meeting with Hasselbourg had been on a Saturday evening, August 30th. The season for bear opened the following Monday. Another lucky break, or perfect timing, as Pete and I chose to call it! At this time of year, Hasselbourg assured us, the creeks were full of salmon, and the bears came down to the creeks to feed on the salmon. We were to do our hunting by wading up the creeks.

"What have you got to wear on your feet?" he inquired, looking dubiously in their direction.

"Sneakers," we replied with as much assurance as we could muster. We were both wearing sneakers; how much equipment did he think a Moth could carry?

"You'll get wet," he suggested.

From his description of hunting conditions, this sounded plausible enough; but what was there to do about it?

"Those things won't last," he continued pointing scornfully at our dainty sneakers. Hunting wild Kodiak bear in Alaska in sneakers and golf stockings did seem a little incongruous. There is always something about a big leather boot that gives the feeling of greater strength and manliness. I feel sure I could approach a bear with more confidence in riding boots than in bare feet or even sneakers. But on the other hand, if it came to taking my departure rather unexpectedly, I should prefer sneakers. In any case, sneakers were all we had so, I believe for the first time in the history of big game hunting in Alaska, sneakers became the official foot gear of an expedition.

During dinner we made plans. Hasselbourg, with his customary independence and lack of sympathy for government bureaucracy, had not renewed his guide's license. We decided, however, this was not important for a few days, because if we should meet a particularly large bear, we could always shoot in self defense; or who could say that Hasselbourg had not done the killing. As a result of recent legislation there was nothing to restrict residents of Alaska from shooting grizzlies and Kodiaks, or Alaskan brown bear, as they are called in the statutes.

Less than a year before our visit, a forest ranger from Juneau had disturbed a sleeping Kodiak not far from Hasselbourg's camp and fired three bullets at him. The ranger was carrying an old rifle and shooting steel-jacketed bullets. He should never have fired or even gone into the woods with such a gun, for it is well known that steel-jacketed bullets will not stop these bear. A bear's first instinct is to run but, of course, the wounded bear charged and killed the ranger and the Alaskan Legislature concluded these monarchs of the forest were becoming too numerous and too dangerous and so removed all restrictions against the natives shooting them. According to the best authorities with whom we talked, it was a great pity as it may result in the extermination of these rare animals.

It was arranged that early the following morning, we should hunt by camera. We would not use our guns unless charged upon, or unless we should meet an unusually large bear, in which case—well, we would wait until the occasion arose.

Hasselbourg told us that he himself had not killed a bear for seventeen years. Yes, he had fired at a few in self defense. Just a few days before our arrival, he and his nephew had been hunting eagles and on their way back to camp met a bear head on. The trail was narrow, and the bear "acted ugly." Not taking any chances with only a shotgun, Hasselbourg waited until the bear was close, then let him have it in the eyes. The bear rose, put both paws up to its eyes, bawled, snorted, and ran off down the trail. Another time he had fired from a rowboat on Hasselbourg Lake when chased by a swimming bear. "You must visit Hasselbourg Lake. It is just a few miles up the creek and there you will find some of the best trout fishing in the world. You can land there easily in your plane." So the stories ran—and to think that for two weeks this fairyland was to be our life.

The comfort of the little stove, the plans of the old man and his stories of Alaska should have kept us awake for hours, but flying all day in an open plane over new and exciting country had its soporific effect. Soon after supper Pete and I were ready to turn in.

Outside it was clear, cool, but not cold. The fragrant odor of evergreens and cedars permeated the night air. The sound of jumping salmon rose above the more regular splashing of the creek.

"Another clear day tomorrow," said Hasselbourg with a tone of disgust as he lowered the door for the night. "We haven't had any kind of real weather for weeks."

I crawled inside a sleeping bag dressed in my BVD's and a fur-lined flying suit. My bed was a thin mattress thrown upon the floor of the living room. Although the window was opened a little, both the door and window were barred to keep out straying animals. Hasselbourg, his nephew and Pete slept upstairs in the attic.

XXI

The Hunt

I MUST HAVE FOUND the sleeping conditions to my liking, as it seemed only a few minutes from the time I threw myself on the floor until I saw Hasselbourg crouched in the dim morning light whittling shavings to start a fire.

Much to his disappointment, the nephew was not allowed to go with us. He was left to fish in the creek, with careful instructions to take his gun with him whenever he went out and not to go beyond sight of the cabin.

According to schedule, the cool draft of early morning air was coming down the creek so there was no chance of the bears getting our scent. We started right up the creek which flowed past the cabin, walking in single file, Hasselbourg leading, Pete in the middle and I bringing up the rear. After following the near bank for 100 yards around the first sharp bend above the cabin, Hasselbourg struck across the swift stream. With his boots pulled high he went into the water almost up to his waist, occasionally placing the butt of his gun against a protruding boulder to aid his balance in the strong current. I felt sorry for my sneakers, and more sorry for myself, but there was nothing to do but follow as best I might. Those first few steps I will not soon forget. First my feet were numbed; then cold and wet above the knees, I slipped off a shiny boulder and was wet almost to the waist. It seemed like ice around my legs. Was this bear hunting? I had had enough to last me a life time.

Up a steep bear trail the old guide led us, around a waterfall and down the other slope. We were almost running to hold the old man's pace. From the uneven trail of fallen trees and soft moss, I was casting quick glances into the thick foliage on either side, expecting to see a huge bear glaring through. Then we made another diagonal crossing of the creek, but this time the water was only knee deep and not so icy. The clamber up the hill had warmed us, our blood was coursing faster and, after stumbling along another hundred yards of rocky river, we had become quite accustomed to the water. That first plunge was painful but the water, though chilly, was not really icy. Our attempts to keep up with Hasselbourg as he shuffled along with his quick, short steps over the rough river bottom kept us keyed for the sport.

We could not have been gone more than three-quarters of an hour when Hasselbourg, a few yards ahead, turned and hissed, "Sst—here's a bear."

For every conscious minute since landing at Admiralty Island I had fully expected to see a bear suddenly appear before me; for the last three-quarters of an hour I had been sneaking in search of one, every now and then raising my gun for a practice aim at an imaginary beast. But this sudden "Here's a bear" caught me quite unprepared. I fumbled and all but dropped my gun. Regaining my composure, I looked around the bend in the creek and, sure enough, in real life, there walked a bear!

"He's just a three-year old," our guide informed us. What a relief! He was too young to shoot! All we had to do was watch, as with his rolling gait, he ambled upstream swinging his head from side to side in search of salmon. Finally he disappeared through the underbrush, his search unsatisfied.

Not only had we reached Alaska, we had seen a bear. Perhaps all this would not suprise our doubting friends when they read about it in our science notebook!

On approaching the spot where we had first seen Bruin, we concluded he had not fished in vain, for there on the rocky shoals in the center of the creek were the disgusting remains of several salmon. In some cases there was little left but the head and bones; in others, just a bite had been taken from the cheek or hump, and the fastidious diner had gone in search of a more delicate morsel.

As far as the salmon went up the creek there were signs

of recent feeding by the bears, and occasionally we saw wet tracks on the bars at the side or middle of the creek. Of course, one bear might have left several tracks but we must have seen a dozen different tracks on our first trip that morning.

Possibly another hour of wading, then—

"Sst—here are some bear." I remember even in the excitement of the moment the use of the plural amused me. What sort of game preserve was this? After several days of search I had dared to hope we might see one bear. Could this be true? Yet, sure enough! There around the bend less than a hundred yards away were a mother and two little cubs playing in the water.

"Get your camera—here's your chance to get a picture," whispered Hasselbourg. I say "whispered," but he did not whisper. He talked in a low, melodious tone that seemed to blend into the sounds of nature. A whisper, he said, was far more easily noticed by game.

Unfortunately, I had the camera, so reluctantly I handed Pete my gun and, camera aimed, I started toward "Ma" bear and cubs. Considering the footing, I was quite proud of my steady progress when I seemed to hear a "back-seat driver." "Go steadily and they won't notice you." It was Hasselbourg's low voice. Fearfully I proceeded faster, wondering why the bears were not noticing a full grown man approaching down the middle of the creek.

"Go faster. You can get much closer; they won't run." It was Hasselbourg again. What fool advice! I recalled that Ernest Thompson Seton, or was it Ernest Seton Thompson, had advised me as a boy that a mother bear with cubs was better left alone. But by this time I was mad and taking one quick backward glance at Pete, that disagreeable guide and my treasured rifle, I strode boldly toward Mrs. Bear and young.

I was not more than thirty yards away. It flashed through my mind that I could have passed a football over the bears as they continued playing in the stream. Did Hasselbourg expect me to go up and join the play? But now Ma Bear had noticed callers and towering to her full height her huge paws raised level with her head, she eyed me critically. She looked mountain-high as she stood before me.

"Time to run! Time to run!" I told my legs. Would they never get the message? "I want to be somewhere else." While my legs were trying to function, Mother Bear dropped lightly to all fours and after two quick steps leapt up the bank to watch her cubs and me from behind a huge tree trunk.

"She's going to wait and see what you do with the cubs," Hasselbourg explained from the rear.

I had only one desire in life—to show the mother I intended to do nothing with her cubs. My legs were beginning to understand my wishes better so I quickly joined my battery a short distance back. After playing together a few seconds, the cubs ran to join their mother and we heard the family crashing off through the forest.

Even Hasselbourg admitted she was a fair-sized bear. "Oh, she might have stood nine feet but you could see her fur was bad. And if you killed her, the cubs would never live. Some big bear would eat them."

The cubs probably stood two feet high when on all fours and were quite fat and rolly. They were the smallest cubs we saw during our visit on the island.

Unfortunately these moving pictures did not come out well. Perhaps the camera was shaking too violently, but in self defense I must add that it was misting at the time; the day was dark and the arch of thick foliage above the creek left the bears in comparative shadow. Unfavorable light was one of the principal difficulties with our animal photography because, although seldom raining, it was often overcast and cloudy and many of our best subjects were taken in deep shade.

The best way to take photographs is to select a likely fishing ground where the light is good, then find a sheltered blind down-wind and wait for the bears to come. We found such a shelter behind an upturned tree root right at the junction of two creeks where we waited for two hours but no bears came to our studio that day.

With only four short days to hunt it seemed like wasting time to lie in wait for an occasional bear when by walking up-stream we could meet a number of them. Even by photographing in this way, we did obtain some good close-ups of bears catching salmon.

At Ketchikan we had been told how the bears scoop and even bat the salmon from the streams onto the banks. Hasselbourg denied this and said in all his years he had never seen a bear scoop a salmon. Our observations confirmed Hasselbourg's. We saw several bear pounce on salmon or strike them with their paws, then pick them up in their mouths and walk to the sand bar or bank to enjoy their feast. Our motion pictures show this clearly but as this is not the scientific record of our trip, I shall refrain from starting up any controversy.

We went along the creek that first morning as far as the salmon were running, a distance of about four miles. When the early morning breeze shifted, the wind came up the creek so that we were able to hunt down stream all the way back to camp.

It was after one when we returned to the cabin and, with appetites whetted by having seen four bear in one morning, our stomachs were crying for food. The meat larder was empty.

"Let's have some fresh fish for lunch, boys. Go out and catch one of those cohoes in the pool beside the cabin."

The hump backed salmon are not considered good eating after entering the streams. But the cohoes are a much larger fish and considered quite a delicacy. A few cohoes had already started upstream, and we had noticed several that morning. With a good stout fishing pole, a heavy cod line and halibut hook, Pete and the nephew marched out to provide our lunch and I followed with the camera to see the fun. A large cohoe was soon spotted, and after two or three casts Pete hooked him by the tail. I was aiming the camera at the fish jumping out of the water when suddenly I heard a shout and looked around just in time to see Pete disappearing head first into the pool. Pete having poised on a narrow ridge found the salmon too much for him. It meant losing the fish or going in, and Pete went in, wearing his only suit of clothes. I swung the camera just in time to get Pete emerging from his bath.

By two o'clock we were eating a delicious cohoe salmon and Hasselbourg and I agreed that it was well worth getting Pete's clothes wet. Hasselbourg's estimate that the salmon weighed twenty pounds seemed conservative to me.

As a fisherman, Pete was irrepressible. Directly after lunch Pete borrowed some of Hasselbourg's finery and went off with the nephew to a nearby trout stream. Hasselbourg was devouring the newspaper we had brought him from Ketchikan and I was entering statistics in our scientific notebook when Pete came tearing back to camp. A bear had come right down the stream where they were fishing! They deemed it wise to resign their positions amicably and Pete came running back for a gun. Thereafter we never went fishing without such protection.

Late that afternoon we saw two more bear up the creek and took some movies of them.

"Just cubs," Hasselbourg described them, but if these were "just cubs," I was beginning to lose my interest in full grown bear.

"Seven bear seen the first day; not bad," I commented at dinner.

"The kid and I have done so much shooting for eagles the last three weeks, all the big bear are frightened away. They're wise old fellows." This was the only comment Hasselbourg would make.

Dinner was soon over. "Alaska; seven bear the first day." With these thoughts I fell asleep.

XXII

Flight to Juneau

MONDAY WE AROSE a little earlier. Having seen so many fresh tracks on the way up the creek the morning before, we decided we had started a little late. This day we wanted to see the bear themselves so we started up the creek about 6:30 a. m. Again the chilly first plunge! Our feet were wet for another sixteen hours or so, until we dried them out between the blankets that night.

This day was almost a repetition of the first. I began to think that our luck could not continue. Seven bears the first day! Why, I had friends, real game hunters too, who had been to Admiralty Island for two weeks without seeing a single bear. I had no particular desire to kill a bear, but we had come to Alaska to hunt them, and paid $50 for our licenses. Under the new law, giving the natives unlimited shooting rights, great Alaskan brown bear might soon be extinct, so this might be our last chance. How dreadful— our last chance! Yes, I *could* remember the time when going through life without shooting a Kodiak bear would have been an endurable prospect, but somehow the shooting of a bear had become the measure of the success of our expedition. What friends would believe us if we told them that we could have shot a bear, but did not, because we were waiting to get a big one. Yes, we must shoot at least one. So Pete and I talked until we were in such a state we were determined to shoot the very next bear regardless of its size.

In a few minutes an unsuspecting ursus horribilis (used for variety's sake, but meaning a grizzly or brown bear) poked his head through the bushes beside the creek in which we were standing. Hasselbourg as usual had spotted him

77

first although he could not have been thirty yards from us. Ursus's right shoulder and front leg were in full view, and Hasselbourg had said if a bear stood side view to shoot him in the shoulder. Fully resolved to act, I quickly put gun to shoulder and took aim; the bear was so close I felt I could not miss. But it seemed cruel. Ursus seemed so peaceful and innocent and still unmindful of our presence as he looked up the creek.

"A great bear hunter you are," I was saying to myself as Pete broke the silence.

"Hasselbourg says he's just a small one; we'll see bigger ones."

That was an idea, and with a feeling of distinct relief I brought down my gun. What was there sporting about shooting at such a target?

As we talked it over Ursus saw us and withdrew his head. We heard the bushes splinter as he charged off through the "jungle," sounding far from the peaceful monarch he had looked a few seconds earlier.

Then Pete and I began to wonder. Had not we just agreed the next bear should be shot? What if it were an easy target? We had to take home a bear. Our pride and our public demanded one.

"This guy Hasselbourg," I said, "is trying to make a nice little bear sanctuary out of his backyard. These bear are not so small. He says they are, just so we won't shoot them, and he can show his pets to future hunters."

We agreed the next bear would be ours before Hasselbourg could stop us.

Thus pondering, we rounded a bend in the creek and almost stumbled on a mother bruin jumping from the creek on to the bank followed by a two-year old cub. They were out of sight before we had a chance to shoot. We waited a few minutes to peer around the shoulder of the hill which bordered the creek, expecting the bears to return to the water for more fishing. They did not return, however, so we started down the stream. Suddenly there was a loud commotion and up jumped mother bear and cub from the very place on the bank where we had seen them disappear. Forsaking their catch of salmon they were off again, this

time into the impenetrable forest. Had we been more
patient, the bears would doubtless have returned to the
creek for more salmon and we should have had a perfect
shot. It was well for us Hasselbourg had not overheard our
resolution to shoot the next bear, but we let the resolution
stand.

Back at the cabin we had another late lunch. It was
now Monday afternoon, September 2nd. Two weeks from
the following day we were due back in Boston, and Boston
seemed a long way off. Our hunting days were getting short,
so we decided to fly to Juneau that day and try to get
Hasselbourg's license renewed. Pete hated to leave our
gaming paradise, but since Hasselbourg refused to go with
me in the air, Flit's crew stuck together. Although he had
never been up and did not relish the idea, Hasselbourg did
agree that if we could not obtain the renewal without his
being present, he would fly over to help us out. We might
not have been so conscientious about his having a license
but it was against the law to hunt without a licensed guide
and should we shoot a bear, we should need an affidavit
from this guide in order to get the skin through the customs.

The tide was now low, and it would be after five before
Flit could float down the creek. A whole afternoon could
not be wasted, so Pete and I went up the side creek and lay
in wait where the bear had disturbed Pete's fishing the day
before. But the bear did not return.

As soon as the tide permitted, we had Flit under way and
taxied out of the channel. Although he never said a word,
we knew from his expression that the nephew longed to go
along and we were sorry Flit could carry only two. The old
man watched our every move always insisting that his outboard was good enough for him He boasted about his
engine, and I boasted of ours. True to habit Flit sustained
the boast and started on the first swing of the prop.

For Hasselbourg, it was 125 miles in his outboard to
Juneau, a long day's run. For us it was only 70 miles airline
flying up the so-called Seymour Canal and overland across
the Indians' canoe "carry" at the neck of the peninsula. If
we could possibly get his license renewal in time and the

evening stayed light, we intended to be back that night. We hated to waste time away from Admiralty Island.

It seemed natural to be in the air again. The Seymour Canal was almost rippleless; the air seemed thick with ducks and geese, and as we flew low above the water we noticed its smooth surface was occasionally broken by seals. On one sandy point Pete saw a bear, so we circled, but the bear disappeared. Since we had a rifle, we were prepared to land if sufficiently tempted.

As we neared Juneau, thick clouds enshrouded the mountains on either side of the passage leading up to the town and we could see poor weather ahead. Within twenty miles of the city we ran into mist and rain. It grew quite dark as we flew low under a cloud and our windshields clouded so that we had to poke our heads outside. Then, of course, the rain caught us squarely in the face and we could see little more. With wretched visibility we barely skimmed the water as we flew past the city and landed just beyond the coal wharves. Fog-flying is no fun especially when it is getting dark. We were not sorry to be down.

No flying back to Hasselbourg's that night! With the help of Hayes and Larry Parks of the Alaska Washington Airways Company, we tied up for the night. They had heard about us by radio from Ketchikan and wondered where we had been.

Uptown the Gastineau Hotel was filled. The salmon season, the best in the history of Alaska, was about over and all the fishermen were back in town. The Alaska Washington men, however, insisted upon looking after brother flyers, and two of them promptly doubled up and gave us one of their rooms. They introduced us all around and entertained us in true Alaskan style. They urged us to go to the ball that night. We apologized for the only clothes we had, and Pete looked dubiously at the knee of my well worn breeches, not too securely held together by a string. "Hell, you're in Alaska now." So we accepted.

The music was good, the girls were as gay and friendly as the men and before the night was through, the conservative Boston flyers were on first names with Juneau's entire dancing population. We were interested to find the girls

well and quite snappily dressed, some in shirt waists and
skirts and others in simple afternoon dresses and, if a little
over made up, on the whole we agreed they were far from
unattractive.

Alternating mist and heavy rain in the morning made Mole
Harbor seem a long way off. Win Goddard, the very obliging
Game Commissioner, helped us obtain the renewal of Hasselbourg's license and then showed us where to do our shop-
ping about town. We were particularly interested in looking
at silver fox skins. Although we had not expected to meet
trappers giving them away in the streets, still $275 to $400
for a good one did seem high in Alaska. We explained that
elsewhere in the world there was a business depression and
assured them that in a year if we returned we would be
able to buy their unsold skins at half this price. At that,
I guess we must have been conservative. Instead, we pur-
chased trinkets made from walrus tusks.

By noon, though raining still, the sky was brighter. As
they said it might be clearer a few miles south of the harbor
entrance, we planned to start back right after lunch.

While lunching at the restaurant, a stranger inquired of
us if we were the boys that were flying over to Hasselbourg's.
He then asked if we would mind taking over a telegram
that had just come in for Hasselbourg. We assured him that
we should be glad to furnish the quickest radio delivery
Mole Harbor had ever had. Radioed from Seattle about
noon, delivered at Mole Harbor the same afternoon! This
was quite a contrast to occasions when mail and telegrams
had waited months in Juneau for Hasselbourg to come to
town. One bad winter he told us he had lived six months
on the island without once going to town or seeing a human
face. We asked him how he stood it. Oh, living alone had
never bothered him. There was always plenty to occupy
oneself. He had had three partners at different times since
living on the island, but that did not work so well. Two
of them had gone crazy and he had had to take them over
to the mainland. There were other questions we longed to
ask, but could not.

It was still drizzling as we cast off from Juneau and headed
south down the Gastineau Channel. At the channel entrance

the weather cleared, although on looking back we could see the same wet clouds hanging around the mountains on either side of Juneau. We swung east over the Taku Inlet and flew above the famous glacier of that name. Taku Glacier extends inland up the river bottom many miles; we were told 300. At its mouth the glacier is about three miles broad and the sea wall of sheer ice rises two to three hundred feet above the water. Like an iceberg, its greatest proportions are under water. Honeycombed with deep crevasses, it was an awesome picture from the air. As far as the eye could see, the glacier shone, a sea of troubled ice with glistening peaks and ridges.

There is little wonder visitors get the idea that Alaska is a rainy spot. Ketchikan, where many tourists stop, is situated on the steep shore of an island with a 3400-foot mountain for a background and a narrow channel separating it from another mountainous island opposite. Ketchikan, according to the Weather Bureau has the second largest precipitation in the world. A few days after my return to Boston, I was to read that seven inches of rain had fallen in Ketchikan in the previous twenty-four hours. Juneau also is on a narrow channel with a 5000-foot mountain rising abruptly behind it and a 3300-foot hill just across the channel. When the warm Japan current makes in against the base of the snow-capped mountains and the glaciers, clouds are formed and when these surround the highlands, they condense and rain falls. On Admiralty Island, however, we had very little rain. It was often cloudy and overcast and occasionally it drizzled. Although the rainy season was just beginning, Hasselbourg had complained there had been no real rain for weeks. Yet sometimes while it was clear at Admiralty, we could see the clouds in the north and suspected that Juneau was being drenched.

Flying arouses interest in cloud formations and makes one realize how strictly local the rain often is. Were I to build a summer home among these islands, as I suspect people will be doing soon to fly up for their vacations, I should study carefully the layout of the hills and pick a spot that was not usually cloaked in clouds.

XXIII

Misses

BACK AT MOLE HARBOR, we circled the camp and waved before landing. Hasselbourg and the boy came running down to meet us and, although away less than twenty-four hours, we greeted one another like old friends after a long separation. By some extraordinary chance Pete's and my feet were quite dry at 4:00 o'clock p.m., a record for the island, so Hasselbourg waded out and with no apparent effort carried us piggy-back fashion to the beach. He then told us that he had once carried two men across a rushing creek, but had refused to assist a woman of the party in like manner.

"I don't want anything to do with them," he muttered. From other remarks we had already classed him as a woman-hater, but this was his strongest condemnation of the opposite sex.

The first night we spent at the cabin, we had offered him a "touch of Scotch" brought from Prince Rupert. "No thanks—never again. I haven't touched a drop for years."

We concluded neither wine nor women were to his liking. Not that we had any reason to connect the two!

The wind was right for bear, and we still had time to do the four miles of the creek. Splashing up the stream again seemed like old times after the day of softening city life.

It was after dusk when we returned that evening. For some minutes we had proceeded in silence, weary from our hurried tramp. I was clambering up the steep track, supporting myself by the protruding roots of overhanging pines, when Hasselbourg's low voice broke the silence.

"Well, that's the first time in three years that during the salmon season I've been up and down that creek without seeing a single bear. We'll have to go to Bear Creek in the morning."

We did not doubt him. During our visit this was the only time we went up any creek with Hasselbourg without sighting at least one Kodiak or grizzly. We asked how many bears he thought there might be on the island.

"That's pretty hard to say, but there are plenty. One evening in the uplands with your friend, Harold Coolidge, we saw twenty-seven within three hours' time. You can ask him, as I think he will remember." On my return I asked Harold and he thought Hasselbourg was wrong, as he had counted only twenty-six.

The next two days were spent much as before, except more strenuously, as Pete and I were getting in better condition; Hasselbourg seemed never to tire. We varied our routine and did several different creeks, and if the wind was wrong, we would go inland through the maze of forest made almost impassable by the clinging undergrowth. At times the footing was swampy; at times there was only one passage along the trunks of huge fallen trees; and at other times the cliffs were steep with little support for hands or feet, but by far our toughest enemy was the huge plant, devil club, with its long thorns on stems and backs of leaves. That Hasselbourg led us unerringly through all this backland without a sign of trail, without compass and without sun, bore testimony to his woodcraft. By some miracle we would come out abruptly into the daylight and find an expanse of rolling fields covered with blueberry patches and cut by bear tracks and paths. During these highland expeditions, although twice we heard a bear receding at the noise of our approach, we never saw one. All the bears we saw were at the creeks.

After our sojourn in the uplands, we came down Mole Harbor Creek. Since our return to Admiralty Island, we had not seen a bear, but our determination was still strong. We had even left our cameras at the camp. This expedition had been to shoot a bear. As Pete was the hunter of the trip, I had insisted that he take the first shot.

Walking from a stony shoal into the creek, Hasselbourg raised his hand. "Here's one." And up the stream there came a bear. With his head low and swinging from side to side, he shuffled towards us in a foot of water, running as if chasing the fish upstream. It was an end-on target, perhaps 100 yards away and far from stationary. With Hasselbourg's first signal Pete had fallen flat upon his stomach on the stony sloping shoal. He took aim and fired. I may have shut my eyes, but anyhow I, too, fired. The bear turned for the bank, and they said he was out of sight when my gun reported. Perhaps he was, but there were two marks close together in the tree behind the place where Bruin had been playing.

Pete could not understand it. He offered no excuses, but cajoled himself in no uncertain terms. Personally I should have been dumbfounded if I had hit that swinging target. Hasselbourg said we were not the first ambitious easterners to find a bear was not such an easy target as his size would lead one to believe. He muttered to himself and I decided it was just as well I had not understood him. Pete walked dejectedly back to the shoal, from which we had fired to figure out how such misses were possible.

"Never lie down when shooting at a bear, especially on a downhill lie like that," cautioned Hasselbourg. "Prone shooting may be all right for target practice, but for game it's much better just to sit and use your knees for a rest."

I could not help but be amused and chortled to myself with malicious delight. This was Pete's first shot. Up to this minute I had had little hope of killing my first bear unless the target came and licked my gun. Now that Pete had missed his, I should not feel so badly if I missed mine. With increasing confidence I imagined how perfect it would be for me to hit my first and I grew eager for the chance.

Pete now took up the rear and I trailed Hasselbourg. I took quick practice aims at trees and stumps and sat on rocks now and then to get the sitting posture. If I simply held back until the bear was in the sights, I began to feel I could not miss.

From the moment of Pete's failure, Hasselbourg kept telling us of other famous misses by noted visitors. He told us who they were, how wide they had missed and what they had said. This gave him great amusement and I hesitate to think how we added to his list of stories.

Having reached the mouth of Mole Harbor Creek without further signs of bear, we took the "outboard" over to Bear Creek.

"Here they're apt to run a little bigger than on the Mole Harbor Creek," he warned.

We landed on the high sand bar which extends into the Seymour Canal from the south side of the Creek. The nephew paddled around in the boat shooting at seals with a .22 while we went wading up the creek.

"Go carefully here. I've seen bears at the mouth of this creek."

Over the sand bar we went, and we were hardly in the mouth when Hasselbourg almost shouted: "Quick, there's a big one."

It seemed a long way up the creek to the spot where we saw the hind quarters of a bear receding from us. He had not seen us, and I started to hurry along the bank to get a closer shot.

"The wind's shifted," Hasselbourg called. The wind was fluky at the entrance to the creek. "You'll have to shoot quickly or he'll get your scent and be gone."

With thumping heart I took quick aim and fired. Almost instantly Pete's rifle sounded in my ear. I had been convinced the bear was covered with the sights, but at the report of my gun he turned quickly into the deep grass beside the creek. On account of the rocky, slippery footing, I had always found it extremely difficult walking in Mole Harbor Creek. Bear Creek was no different but as if the guns had signalled the start of a hundred-yard dash, I sprinted down the center of the creek as fast as my legs would move. Although Pete had run anchor-man on the Dartmouth relay only four years before, he had hard work passing me. We ran on, unmindful of our footing and ever peering for quarry. Suddenly over the tall grass about forty yards away we saw the bear standing on his hind feet and looking curiously down at us from his great height, a perfect target. Yes, this bear was a big one. We slid to a stop as quickly as possible, but before we could raise our guns the bear had run off through the bushes. We both fired blindly toward the brush, but saw no further traces of that bear, nor did we find any signs of blood. Just one more inexcusable miss.

Hasselbourg, not the kind to listen to our excuses, said the bear was not over 100 yards away, an easy shot. I insisted he was much farther and for my satisfaction paced it off; 125 yards was the best I could make it.

Bear Creek seemed well named, although this was the only ursus we saw that morning. "That bear was only about three feet across the rear," Hasselbourg consoled us. "I'll take you over to Pleasant Bay where they're so broad you can't miss them. Also, you'll get more shots at them because there are lots of canyons there, and when the bears feel boxed, you'll have them coming toward you, instead of running away."

This sounded interesting.

In spite of Hasselbourg's boasting about his outboard, the engine showed some hesitation in starting. Perhaps it too was a trifle reluctant to meet these bears in canyons. I did not hesitate to remind the proud possessor of a Johnson outboard motor that Flit never behaved that way.

XXIV

Hits

ONCE AGAIN it was to be Pete's shot. We were walking up the south bank of the Pleasant Bay creek to escape some rapids. We had not yet reached the promised canyons. We were treading quietly in single file when Hasselbourg stopped and pointed at the opposite bank about forty yards away. I was following closely and almost tripped on Pete as he wheeled and raised his gun.

"For God's sake hit him, he's a big one," I whispered excitedly. The bear was standing on his hind legs and looked us over in customary bear fashion.

Pete, now realizing bears did not hold this position for long, lost no time in firing. The bear ducked and ran away. Pete and I both fired once again into the brush through which the bear had disappeared.

"Did you have him covered?" asked Hasselbourg. What a question!

"If I didn't, you can shoot me," Pete offered nobly. "I may have been a shade to the left of center."

"When they're hit, they usually bawl out or else fall down. He didn't do either," drawled the old man. "You ought to hit right in the middle when they stand like that, then you break their back, and they cannot run."

I may have been unsympathetic about Pete's first miss, but to hear the prize gunner of our expedition talked to in this way was more than I could stand. "Of course, he hit him," I insisted, not knowing the slightest thing about it.

"Well, stick together anyway. We don't want any wild shooting if there's a wounded bear around."

We waited a few minutes, then crossed the stream and found thick blood drops on the bank, then a small pool of

88

blood on a large leaf of devil club. I did not see how so much blood could have flowed so quickly.

"You hit him all right," drawled Hasselbourg. Then as if regretting even this admission, he added quickly, "Perhaps you got him in the leg. They sometimes bleed badly when wounded in the leg." How unkind!

Under one large windfall and over another the blood trail led us.

"Wounded bears have a way of waiting behind a tree and jumping out as you come by," Hasselbourg warned us, quite unnecessarily, however, as Pete and I were all eyes and ears. With guns carried in both hands for instant use, we followed through the "jungle."

One hundred yards from the bank we came upon the bear lying meekly on her side between two large windfalls, her front legs stretched to full length and her paws resting pathetically one upon the other. Thick blood stains bore testimony that her last effort to surmount a five-foot trunk was crowned with failure as she had fallen back to her present resting place, stone dead.

"Too bad, just a cub," said Hasselbourg as he peered over the first windfall.

"How much do you suppose that little cub weighs?" we queried.

Hasselbourg eyed the body. "Not over 700, but the skin's not bad for a female at this time of year."

The cub was too heavy to be moved, and we skinned her where she lay. I tried to photograph our trophy, but in the shade of the dense woods even a time exposure did not develop.

Skinning a 700-pound bear is no easy task. After completing one side Pete and I tried in vain to roll the carcass over. In the end it took three of us to do it.

When the skinning was completed, Hasselbourg and Pete decided to perform an autopsy and seek the cause of death. Since this was my first experience of the kind, they had been considerate enough not to ask me to skin the head, but even the feet were almost more than I could stand. The padded feet and claws were almost human. I had had enough. Inexperienced at cleaning game and not being a surgeon by profession, I felt in need of fresh air. The "jungle" in the neighborhood of this huge fleshy carcass seemed close and stifling, so I went for a walk among the trees. They called me back.

Hasselbourg held in his hand the huge heart, six or seven inches across cut through the bottom by a hole larger than the average man's wrist. Through this hole, the bullet from Pete's 405 had torn its way and stopped against the vertebrae behind. Proudly Pete exhibited the bullet, which was mushroomed to a full inch in diameter. With this bullet through her heart the bear had turned and run so agilely that Hasselbourg suspected she had not been hit. Before at last collapsing, she had charged over and under the windfalls and through the thick bushes which it took us ten minutes to penetrate.

The newspapers on our return improved our story and related that the bear shot through the heart had charged us for 100 yards. Had this been true, she would have passed us by fifty yards, as she was only that distance away when Pete fired.

That night I entered in our log: "Wednesday, Mole Harbor, Alaska. Pete shot one bear." Our fondest hopes had now been realized. We had flown to Alaska and shot a Kodiak bear. Yet as I dozed off that night I thought, "It would be sort of nice if I could get one too."

XXV

The Silver-Tipped Grizzly

"**H**M, ANOTHER GOOD DAY," grunted Hasselbourg as he sniffed at the weather. Now we knew why he disliked fair weather and wanted rain. The odor from the salmon which had gone upstream, spawned and died was already beyond the pleasant stage. "If we don't get some freshets down this creek to wash away the salmon within a week, it won't be livable. I'll have to move up to my camp on Hasselbourg Lake."

He told us that one year he had taken 6000 salmon from the stream and used them as fertilizer on his garden. He had carted them out by the wheelbarrowful. (He is welcome to that job.) In the spring he had the world's best garden he claimed, and in it he had raised all the familiar garden vegetables and his potatoes had taken the prize at Juneau.

Thursday morning Pete and I went hunting by ourselves, and Hasselbourg remained behind to scrape the skin. It seemed quite bold to us to bear hunt in Alaska without a guide, although I must admit we did not see one. A strange coincidence, we thought; we did not see a single bear, although when Hasselbourg was with us we had never failed to see one.

For the afternoon, Pete and I added two more creeks to our program.

"You fellows don't seem to know when you've had enough. Most people are satisfied with one and here you're doing three creeks a day." Not that Hasselbourg was tired; we could not tire him.

"Sure, but most people are here three times as long; we're getting three months into one."

I have said the old man spotted every bear ahead of us

91

but this time his instinct was uncanny. We were coming
down Bear Creek. He sniffed.

"Watch out," he murmured, "there's a bear not far away."

We scanned both banks carefully, and followed Hasselbourg. He pointed ahead. Fast disappearing up the hill
was my chance of bringing home a bear! He was running up
the left bank where it rose steeply, seventy-five yards away.
Trees were small and the undergrowth was light. Mindful
of Pete's shining example, I took quick aim and fired at the
rapidly retreating hind quarters. Either I furnished him
with additional momentum, or he turned to give Pete a
better shot, for he veered sharply to the right. Pete added
his lead to mine; the bear's hind quarters were boosted
further up the hill, but at right angles to his original course.
Now he was running down the bank! The excitement was
intense! I ran down stream to get a closer shot. Another
shot from Pete and the poor beast, with no strength to escape
uphill, charged towards us down the bank. Whether his
intent was hostile I shall never know. Neither his attitude
nor his course appeared friendly at the time, but I suspect
he was following the line of least resistance and going down
hill was easier than going up. My most vivid recollection
is one of constant shooting. It sounded like a world war.
Rifle reports echoed from bank to bank. Still forty yards
away, bruin collapsed, too full of lead to continue life's
struggle, and with a crash he rolled down the bank and
landed in the stream at my feet, quite dead.

"Another cub," said Hasselbourg as he came up, "and
what a lot of shooting!"

In our excitement neither knew how many shots he had
fired. Pete was sure of having fired at least four and I
remembered three. We must have fired more, for in the skin
we found eight holes, and one bullet had passed through his
guts and gone out the other side.

This bear, a silver tipped grizzly, really was a cub compared with some we had seen. Hasselbourg estimated his
weight at around 500 pounds but to my mind his lack of
size was largely compensated for by his beautiful fur, with
its silver marking around the neck and back.

Skinning the bear was a good two hours' job and it was

Lombard and "Old Hasselbourg" Take a Brief Respite

At Last a Bear, But Then Comes the Job of Skinning It

The Hunt: Lombard
And Hasselbourg

Pete Emerging
From His Bath

dark before we returned to camp. Heavy clouds sped rapidly across the sky and gave us intermittent glimpses of the moon and stars as we plodded wearily up the creek to the cabin. The barometer had fallen considerably since noon.

Hasselbourg was quite encouraged. "Looks better," he grunted as we sat down to supper. "The wind's working around to the westward and we're pretty sure to get a storm out of this. It may not arrive for a couple of days, but when it does, it's apt to last for several days."

This might be good news to him, but it was quite the reverse for us. Hunting would be out of the question, and we would be confined to the island until the storm blew over. Already our fondest hopes had been satisfied. We had flown to Alaska and each had shot a bear.

"If we are marooned for five days on the island, we can never reach Boston within our allotted month's vacation. The sooner we leave Admiralty, the better. Perhaps it is already too late."

"Yes, but I'd like to get one really big brown bear while I'm up here," Pete protested.

"And I'd like to fly up the coast and see Mt. Fayerweather. It would take only about an hour and a half, and McKinley isn't far beyond," I countered. "We could fly inland and land on a lake at the foot of one of those mountains."

It rained some during the night, but in the morning the barometer was up a little, and the clouds more broken. We were tempted and succumbed to one last hunt at Bear Creek. The search for the "really big bear" was a failure, however.

XXVI

Homeward Bound

At NOON the barometer had again started falling, and there was a strong northwest wind. We dared tempt fate no longer, and at 2:40 that Friday afternoon we taxied out across the choppy surface of Mole Harbor, swooped low over the cabin and reluctantly waved farewell to Hasselbourg and Raymond.

Flying before the strong tail breeze, we rapidly retraced our course around islands and through straits with strange Russian names, to Wrangel. Our progress was so rapid that before reaching Ketchikan, we had made plans to fly on that night to Prince Rupert and partake of the promised celebration with Harry at the Imperial Oil dock. If he had gone home for the night, we could fly over to his camp and tie up on the same mooring as his outboard. We planned without considering the United States Customs, however.

As we came in to land at Ketchikan, we saw the ripple of a squall on the water ahead. The squall struck us, and we dropped almost to the water. It was treacherous landing, and we were greatly relieved to feel the pontoons pounding gently on the ruffled surface.

We landed at five o'clock, a two hours and twenty minutes flight from Mole Harbor. I hurried up to the customs' office. One officer had just gone off duty, so I telephoned the officer coming on at 5:00. He was having supper and informed us curtly, he would leave his house at six o'clock to come to the office, and not before.

"Yes, but we are very anxious to get to Prince Rupert tonight, and if we have to wait until 6:30, it will be seven before we can get away, and we can't possibly make the 100 miles to Prince Rupert before dark."

"I'll be up soon after 6:oo. I don't intend to have my supper interrupted. You can fly all night as far as I'm concerned."

How obliging! And what a contrast with the customs' officers in British Columbia! Perhaps we were unreasonable, but we had been spoiled by previous friendly treatment. Reluctantly we walked back to cover Flit for the night.

At the dock, Jim Dodson, Pilot of one of the Alaskan planes had just landed with three prospectors whom he had flown to an inland lake in the mountains and had called for after three weeks. This journey on foot, the only other possible means of travel, would have consumed a month each way. The prospectors had accomplished in one month what otherwise would have taken three.

Jim had been presented with a large venison steak, and as his wife was having only one friend for dinner, he urged us to help them eat it. Here once more was the hospitality which had quite spoiled us throughout our trip. We felt we were back in the flying fraternity again and gladly accepted Jim's invitation and stretched it to include a bath and shave before dinner. We had been away from Ketchikan less than a week, but with months of adventure crowded into that week, there was much to tell those friends who had encouraged us on our voyage.

By morning the wind had increased, and it was quite choppy on the narrow stretch of water from which we had to take off. The wind was gusty and variable. A crowd had assembled at the dock to see us start and there was much speculation as to how our plane would behave on such a sea. Our first attempt was a failure. The wind caught the right wing and lifted it until the left was dangerously near the white caps. Cutting the gun, we let the wind blow us back to shelter. On our second try we were careful to head directly into the wind, changing our course to meet it as we came out from the lee of the docks. Flit climbed up on the step of the pontoon, and I shoved the stick forward to gain speed. We were enveloped in a stream of spray as Flit skimmed the water, bounced across a couple of waves and then literally jumped into the air.

Once aloft we realized this northwest wind was not a

local breeze but must have come directly from Bering Strait. As it swooped and swirled between the islands, it developed a variety of currents and made flying very bumpy. Our customs papers were made out for Prince Rupert and we had planned to land and say goodby to Harry. But at the entrance to Prince Rupert Harbor, we could see the town was still blanketed under a thick morning fog. Landing was out of the question when we had a strong tail wind to help us on our way. We had to take advantage of the breeze if we were to have Sunday dinner in Seattle. So we continued south.

A short distance below Prince Rupert we passed a passenger steamer and not far beyond a United States destroyer, both bound south. It was good to see the destroyer roll and realize others too were making heavy weather. We flew low, waved and proudly exhibited the "MASS." written under our wing. "If this representative of the U. S. Navy thinks she is fast, we will show her how the citizens of Massachusetts travel."

At the nearly deserted pulp mill settlement at Swanson Bay, we stopped to refuel Flit and ourselves, and even more important, to pay a $1.60 debt we incurred going north. We had lunch with "the boys" at their camp house. They were mostly Canadians from Vancouver operating the gasoline base and running the camp for the summer.

A young English woman staying there was expecting her husband on the boat from Prince Rupert that day and asked if we had seen the boat. "Yes, almost two hours ago," we replied, "just out of Prince Rupert." That meant it would be almost dark before the boat arrived and by that time we should be well on our way to Victoria and "the States."

A seaplane was based at Swanson Bay, so we inquired of the boys the best altitude for flying.

"Go up to 4000 feet and you'll find it smooth," they counselled. "It's always rough down low when it is windy like this. We're expecting our plane up from Alert Bay some time today. You're in luck. She is having to buck this breeze."

Yes, we were in luck as far as speed was concerned, but not as comfort. From Swanson Bay we climbed to 3000 feet, then 4000, but could not escape the bumps. Although Flit was heavier with pontoons, she still seemed to take an awful tossing. Early that afternoon we saw the Swanson Bay seaplane slowly bucking up between the islands at about the same altitude. She, too, was doing her share of jumping. We climbed another 1000 feet. Five thousand was about our ceiling with pontoons and our load, but the air was just as rough.

As we came down the narrow Finlayson Channel into Milbanke Sound, we decided inland passage flying was too rough for comfort, so out to sea we headed. We watched a steamer down below head eastward through the islands, while we continued southwesterly for the open Pacific. Outside of the islands we could see a broad white rim of surf, and the green Pacific beyond flecked with whitecaps. Away from the mountains the air was smooth, and we dropped to 2000 feet to enjoy the exciting view. The white border underneath took on the shape of churning foam where the big rollers from the northwest crashed against the rocky coast. Had our motor died, landing in those breakers would have been suicide, so we went further out to sea with the idea that if forced down, we could land between the rollers off shore and have a chance to inflate our rubber boat before bouncing in among the rocks.

The steamship lane through the islands was now twenty miles inland, a long walk overland, or an even longer paddle in our rubber boat. But we were cutting corners and in return for the smooth air, we were willing to take some risks. Thus for eighty miles we flew smoothly in a strong breeze above the turbulent Pacific. Then we sighted ominous Cape Caution, the one exposed headland of the inland passage, and twenty miles beyond, the northern end of Vancouver Island gradually took shape. But what terrors did exposed headlands have for us now that flying was steady?

When we flew north in quiet air, we had been proud of our three hours' flying time from Alert to Swanson Bay. This afternoon we had cut an hour from our former time.

Our reception at each familiar port to which we came seemed almost like a home-coming, as our acquaintances in the little outpost towns seemed really glad to welcome us on our return. At Alert Bay, before slipping in to land off the oil dock, we flew along the water front to show them we were back. On the dock Mr. Pitcock and his son were already bringing down gas for Flit. They urged us to stay and have another meal with cordial Mrs. Pitcock. As we climbed the ladder we were met by Mr. Potts, our Customs friend, who was more interested in our success as huntsmen than in our clearance credentials. Our papers had been prepared for Prince Rupert, but since that had been cloaked in fog, we were forgiven and Flit was passed to Victoria.

We explained we could not pay a prolonged visit, as we hoped to make Victoria that night. While Pete attended to the gas, I cleared with Mr. Potts, then ran on to our friend, "Ha, Ha," at the Alert Cafe to get egg sandwiches and ice cream to eat in the air. "Ha, Ha" greeted me with his inimitable chuckle, but as nearly as I could make out from his Oriental laughing mask he was sincerely glad to welcome us again.

Throughout the day we had felt that a storm was steadily overtaking us. Anxious to fly as far as possible before it caught us, we radioed ahead and got the weather report at Victoria. "Partly cloudy, no wind and unlimited visibility." By five o'clock we were off again on our race south.

We would have made Victoria by night and covered 700 miles in our little seaplane that day, but for the delay of circumventing two thunderstorms in Georgia Strait. The wind died soon after we left Alert Bay. The sky blackened in the west and the wind came in ahead. We hugged the shore and flew quite low, thinking that if it really blew, we could land in some sheltered cove. Twice when the rain pelted us like hail, we started to put down, but each time it cleared enough ahead to lure us on. Soon after seven o'clock we circled the well-protected harbor of Nanaimo on Vancouver Island, ninety miles short of our destination, Victoria. Lights were already twinkling in the town, but the shore was shrouded in darkness and the water was so calm that we had to watch our landing carefully. We came in near the beach and saw a buoy ahead. Both beach and buoy served to gauge our landing, and we glided low above the water. There was a sudden twist as we touched the water. Flit veered sharply to the right and almost dipped her wing. For a moment I thought we were going over, but we quickly straightened out and came to a stop. In my care to judge our altitude, I had been too intent on looking out on only one side of the plane. We had landed right wing low; our right pontoon had struck the water first and had almost turned us over.

Nanaimo is a wide open mining town, and this was Saturday night. With the clothes we wore, I think we fitted better at Nanaimo than we would have in Victoria.

Sunday forenoon we flew on to Victoria, and then to Seattle, but it seemed that most of the morning was spent checking through the Canadian and U. S. Customs and Immigration officials. What a lot of red tape for such a little ship! But Flit must have felt very much at home floating beside the Luckenback on Lake Union's crowded waters. After our customs formalities were completed, we flew over to Lake Washington, waved to our friends playing croquet on the terrace, tied up at their private dock and went ashore for tea. We had missed Sunday dinner but our friends were surprised to see us two days early as it was.

That night we took Flit down to Renton Field to have the pontoons taken off and wheels put back. Of all the friends glad to see us on our homeward jaunt, I think Jump Goodwin was the most enthusiastic. It was neither Pete nor I that thrilled him; it was Flit. He seemed as proud of Flit as if she had been the flagship of his fleet. Again he took her into his care and checked her over. The fact that our Gipsy motor never missed a revolution on the homeward trip proves the quality of his loving care.

The spare gas tank was leaking so badly that it was removed for welding. Aluminum welding is a tricky job and the tank was taken into town to one supposed to know about it. Poor man, he did his best, of course, but the tank blew up, and he was taken to the hospital severely burned. We gladly paid him for the repair costs to meet his hospital expenses. Although we never saw the man, he was probably trying to hurry a dangerous job on our account.

We had planned to come home the northern route through Spokane, Montana, North Dakota and so south through Minnesota. This is not a mail route, but it is the shortest way, and we talked with one pilot who had made the trip. He said that it ought to be easy to reach Boston in five days, which would be a day ahead of schedule. Also, the mountains would be lower than those on our journey west. These were all distinct advantages but on the other hand there were several hops of 250 to 300 miles between airports. With only our regular tank, with the chance of head winds and the possibility of getting lost in the mountains, we dared not count on over 250 miles without landing. Once more we studied the maps. Rather than take the time to have a new gas tank made and installed, we decided to come home the southern route through Texas and depend on the safety of shorter hops. So Tuesday afternoon, after two delightful days in Seattle with Pete's friends, the McDermotts, we headed south.

XXVII

Fogbound at Portland

PORTLAND THAT NIGHT and an early start the following day was the plan, but we failed to reckon with Portland fogs. The weather never looked more promising than that evening when we landed at Portland nor did it ever look more discouraging than the following morning when we peered through our hotel window. A soft rain was falling through a dense fog.

An event of the night before at the airport should have forewarned us. The Boeing mail pilots always make the decisions as to whether they will carry passengers or not on their trips. The evening mail south to Redding had been about to leave as we walked through the office. In spite of its being a clear starlit night, the pilot had refused to take passengers because the weather report showed fog in the mountains two hundred miles below. The passengers were complaining of the necessity of taking trains, although the Boeing officials were making all the arrangements for them. Since the pilot was making the trip himself, he must have felt reasonably sure of getting through and it must have been hard to refuse all those impatient passengers. Probably disturbed at having to disappoint them, the pilot neglected to turn on his flying lights before taking off. The starter who checked out the plane noticed this, ran into the office, and picked up the radio telephone transmitter.

"Oh, Harry."

Then a distinct voice from the receiver, "Yes, Joe."

"You didn't turn on your flying lights." Above the end of the field where we heard the roar of the motor, lights flashed on.

"O. K. Joe, thanks."

"O. K., Harry."

This certainly is modern science in practical usage.

We spent the day hanging around the airport, watching the weather reports and hoping for a break which would let us escape. Even the mail trips to the south had been called off but that gave the mail pilots leisure to chat with us, so we felt richly compensated. They talked about land marks to watch for on the next lap of our trip and the places where we might put down.

"There's a good field at Roseburg," one pilot said.

"I'll say there is. That used to be a regular stop for our plane when Jim was on that run. He had a little school teacher friend at Roseburg and at least once a week his plane was forced down there for the night. But she's left now and the mail's more reliable. I don't believe our plane has been in there for months."

"Then there's no point in our stopping at Roseburg," Pete volunteered.

The Boeing pilots on the Seattle to Frisco run are probably among the best mail pilots in the world. The Boeing Company is extremely rigid in its qualifications for mail and passenger pilots, as this is considered one of their most difficult runs. We met the three pilots who took turns on the run. Contrary to our expectations, they were not young men but averaged about forty years. Three thousand hours was the minimum qualification for the job, and all of these men had flown more than 8,000 hours.

At six o'clock the next morning we returned to the field for an early start. It was still foggy and we looked for encouragement. In walked Grover Tyler, our friend with the 12,000 hours to his credit. He had been scheduled to leave at two in the morning for the trip south but had given it up on account of the weather. He was now about to make another try.

"I shouldn't advise you to start," he told us. "It's easy country to get lost in. We've been over it so much that if it clears at all, we can usually place ourselves but I shouldn't consider going if I were you."

We wished him bon voyage and watched him take off

in his big Wasp powered Boeing and climb out of sight
into the fog. What a life! And he with a wife and children!
No wonder he gets $8,000 a year.

Half an hour later as we were sitting in the office there
was a flash on the radio telephone. Joe, the operator, picked
up the receiver.

"Number 3 somewhere over Albany."

"O. K., Grover."

"Say, Joe, if those boys from Boston haven't left yet, tell
them not to. It's rotten. I wish I wasn't here."

"O. K., Grover, thanks," and Pete and I called our thanks
into the transmitter, also. Imagine his taking the trouble to
think of "the boys from Boston" when he must have had
his hands full flying blind for fifty miles of his course and
trying to keep his bearings.

Two hours later, the eight o'clock weather report showed
scattered fog for the 110 miles to Eugene and bad fog further south.

The Western Air Express plane that had put down at
Salem the day before had not come through to Portland
and Salem was only twenty miles south. However, we were
restless because of our enforced delay and decided to go up
and look conditions over. The pilots said there was often
local fog near Salem which could be avoided. At 8:15 we
took off and headed down the river. At Portland our ceiling
was 1,000 feet, but to the westward the hills were blanketed
and twelve miles down the river the fog was thick to the
ground. To carry on was foolish and unnecessary. With
no desire to climb above the fog and be separated from the
ground or to have fog drift in behind and cut off our retreat
to Portland, we turned quickly and flew back along the
river. What would our friends in the Boeing Company who
just waved us good by think of "those fellers who flew to
Alaska" and were scared of a little fog? But not at all; we
were commended heartily for our good judgment.

I am convinced that many accidents occur because of a
pilot's reluctance to turn back. Having decided to make a
start, he hesitates to change his mind. Pride enters in and
once on his way, he is strongly desirous of seeing it through.

Undoubtedly, public opinion and the fear of scorn contribute largely to this point of view. Often in such cases, more nerve is needed to turn back than to fly on against one's better judgment. But after such a choice is made, those very hangers-on at the airport who encouraged him to make the try are the first to commend the careful flyer for his common sense.

Aviation has not yet reached the stage where it is safe to fly in any weather. Everywhere we went we learned of experienced flyers who had crashed in the fog. Usually they had flown into hills or mountains. It is hard enough to keep one's balance in the fog, especially in a small plane, without having to consider collisions with irregularities in the earth's surface, so we decided to eliminate this risk by staying on the ground.

We were back again at the Boeing hangar. Sniff, sniff, a strong smell of gasoline; and then drip, drip. Sure enough, the trailing edge of the upper wing was moist with gasoline. Our main tank must have opened up. Had we only known of the leak the day before while we were waiting in the rain, we could have had it repaired then. Upon investigation, it was not as serious as we had feared. The solder had become loose where the tank had been repaired previously. Draining off the gas and resoldering took up all the morning.

The Western Air Express that put down at Salem on the previous day came in and we talked with the pilot. It was clearing to the southward. Next came the Boeing plane back from Medford with Grover Tyler, pilot. (Tyler was the one who had telephoned not to brave the fog.) "You can make it easily now," he said. "It's a lot better but it was pretty thick this morning." Tyler had been to Medford, exchanged mail with the "Frisco" plane and returned to Portland by one o'clock. The 500 miles finished his day's work, but at 130 miles per hour, it was not such a long day at that.

In the hangar, we saw a new "Mailwing" Boeing monoplane which would cruise at better than 150 miles per hour and which was just being put into use on the mail routes. Even experienced pilots were curious to see Flit, the little Moth, that had flown over the Rockies to Alaska. So Tyler and Tex Rankin, the endurance flyer, and a racing pilot named Smith from the coast, and Les Hubble, Operations' Manager, came out to examine Flit and see us off. Flit, just washed and primed by Boeing mechanics, looked her best.

XXVIII

We Go South

"INTERESTING, BUT UNEVENTFUL," reads our log to Medford. We saw very plainly why they claimed it was easy country in which to get lost. The countless valleys were covered with tall timber and when seen for the first time were almost indistinguishable. The upper air was clear and the clouds were breaking so that when we got into the mountains we could look down through openings in the clouds and still see the timber lands below. Little scenes of mountain peaks and dark green timber lands appeared and reappeared. They formed weird pictures framed by glistening white cloud banks, changing pictures that seemed to portray minature glimpses of a far and distant planet.

"Hello," Pete called through the voice tube. "Have you decided in case the motor quits to jump from here or land in the trees?"

"No. Have you decided which is better?"

"No."

We were above the tall timber of Oregon again, and that question never was settled.

The field at Medford did not look too smooth and inviting, but it was large enough. At one side was a grandstand and a row of buildings; on the ground there was one plane and crowds of automobiles and people. We came down on the rough ground, taxied over near the other plane and were promptly surrounded by a crowd, more curious than cautious.

"Oh, this isn't the airport. This is the fair grounds. The airport is on the other side of town," So over we flew.

At last they were my friends, Tom and Beckie Mills, who came to the field to greet us and take us home for the night.

I had been embarrassed by the number and hospitality of Pete's Dartmouth friends. I had tried to explain that Harvard men travelled more than Dartmouth men and so were always "out of town," but Pete had replied in a patronizing tone that of course Dartmouth men had the greater diversity of interests. So it was a real triumph to find a Harvard graduate and college clubmate chopping trees in the wilds of Oregon.

That evening we learned all about the pear and lumber business and, faithful to the purpose of our expedition, entered the statistics in our scientific notebook:

> "There are 1200 pear crates to a car and during the 1930 season 5,000 cars of pears were shipped from the Medford Valley to New York City at an average price of $2.00 a crate, or a gross business of $12,000,000."

At the Medford hangar, we inadvertently lost our strip map with the course to San Francisco. So we started mapless over the Siskiyou Mountains carrying in our heads the meager directions to Redding which the boys at the hangar had given us. "Cross the mountain range due south at its lowest point; leave snow covered Mt. Shasta on your left and follow the valley about 130 miles to Redding."

The morning air was glorious, crisp and clear as a bell. As we climbed up from Medford, we could see the heavy dew and fog still lying in the mountain passes, though gradually dispersing before the early sun. After crossing the Siskiyous at 7500 feet, we passed close aboard another plane flying north. It was the mail plane bound for Medford, so we knew we were on our course. Pete saw it coming, hurriedly got out the movie camera, turned in the cockpit and snapped a picture as it passed. At an aggregate passing speed of over 200 miles per hour, the plane was not long within camera range. To my later surprise, it did show clearly on the screen, although there were only a few inches of film.

Even before leaving the Siskiyous which lay on the border between Oregon and California, we could see the snow-capped peak of Shasta glistening majestically forty miles ahead. We climbed to 10,000 feet and flew level with the top of one of Shasta's lesser satellites which rose like a cone from the base of Shasta. We circled about, and with this cone as a contrast in the foreground took photographs of Mt. Shasta towering 4000 feet above us.

The field at Redding is on top of a hill and the seemingly large, flat surface is deceptive. True to our training, we circled once to look it over and were very glad we did. It would have been an easy matter to undershoot the field and woe to the pilot who misjudged the altitude and got below the hill where tricky winds and tall trees obstructed his climb. At the weather station, we received good reports ahead. It was a small airport and there were no air maps available, but finally the men at the weather station did offer us their only strip map if we promised to return it. We mailed it back the next day from Los Angeles.

After leaving the mountains, we soon decided central California was a most uninteresting state over which to fly. Perhaps we were prejudiced by the strong head winds with which we had to contend. As we got further south we occasionally ran into strong variable cross-currents which came around the coastal mountains. They seemed to be blowing in directly from San Francisco Bay and made our morning ride far from gentle. At Sacramento we stopped to refuel and then continued for what seemed like hundreds of miles over flat stupid country, about equidistant between the Coast Range and the High Sierras. Late that afternoon we sighted far ahead what looked like a huge encampment of giants. The tall "Pilgrims" or tent-like towers of the oil wells served as an excellent beacon to direct us to the airport at Bakersfield, the "Oil City."

The field was a fine one with tarred runways laid out across that red, dusty soil which so strangely colored all the countryside. If one attempted to turn around off the runways, the dust stirred by the propeller was blinding.

It was almost six o'clock and we wanted to get to Los Angeles that night. "It's only 120 miles over the mountains. You can make it all right before dark," the men at the field said encouragingly. "There are beacons all the way

to Los Angeles and anyhow you can't put down in Los
Angeles without finding yourself in an airport."

"Say, where's your N. C.," called the young official at the
office where we registered. "You can't fly in this state on
a Massachusetts license."

We had almost forgotten we did not have a Federal rat-
ing, it had been so long since this unpleasant subject had
been mentioned.

"Why, this is an emergency landing, and we are just
going through. We shouldn't have thought of coming
through California, but our extra tank blew up and we are
on our way to Los Angeles to get another. You wouldn't
keep us from getting to Los Angeles tonight, would you?"

The official was considerate in interpreting the regulations and in fifteen minutes after our quickest refueling
stop, we were allowed to depart.

Thirty miles south of Bakersfield, the Sierra-Nevada range
swings westward towards the coast. Although only 120 miles
to Los Angeles, more than half the journey is over these
mountains. They are not particularly high, but we had
no desire to fly strange mountains in the dark. We headed
south and climbed steadily for fifteen minutes before reaching the foothills. Ten minutes later we were getting into
real mountains. The sun was low, and the sky had a strange
rosy tint. Already the valleys were in deep shade. We might
have gone forty miles, but that meant eighty to go, or at
least an hour's flying.

"Hello, Pete," I called into the voice tube.

"Hello, yourself."

"I think it's foolish."

"So do I."

Back we went to Bakersfield and spent the evening at
"The Dawn Patrol," learning from the moving picture what
it really was to fly. Although disappointed at not reaching
Los Angeles, we had covered 600 miles that day, not counting our eighty-mile jaunt south of Bakersfield and not counting all the miles we flew behind the German lines that
evening.

"Pete, that flying inspires me," I said as I turned in.

"I think I'll loop to a landing at Hollywood tomorrow." At Hollywood I was expecting to be met by a friend, and not a Harvard graduate, either.

"Good stuff," said Pete. "But do you mind letting me know before you start the loop, so I can bail out and tell her what you are doing?"

The boys at Bakersfield were very much interested in our trip, and when they called to motor us to the field in the morning, they were already making plans for flying to Alaska on pontoons the following summer. But even those enthusiasts seemed to lack confidence in Flit.

"Best of luck," they said, as we shook hands in parting. "Be sure to let us know if you get back to Boston O.K."

Would we ever overcome the skepticism of our friends? The daring feats of "The Dawn Patrol" seemed to have increased our enthusiasm for flying and I think we enjoyed our flight over the San Bernardino Mountains to Los Angeles even more than usual. The morning fog on the western side of the mountains was just burning off as we came over the top of the range. We dipped under the scattering clouds and on coming down the Antelope Valley toward the city of Los Angeles, we saw airports in every direction. There were three huge ones all within gliding distance so we picked the largest and landed at the Glendale Central Airport.

Again the question of our Federal license was brought up but we quickly changed the subject to our gas tank which once more had sprung a leak.

"Could you have it fixed by tomorrow morning, because in two days we are due in Boston?"

It was a Curtiss Service Station and although the Moth was now controlled by the Curtiss-Wright Company, Moths were no longer being built in the United States; the Curtiss employees were not as interested in our ship as strangers throughout the northwest had been. We concluded that California was spoiled by too much flying and that we liked her least of all the states that we had crossed. At last the manager did agree to have our tank fixed by the following morning and our motor checked; we left for other and pleasanter duties in the Golden State.

We were being entertained by Ellen Mead, the attractive daughter of family friends living in Hollywood. Remembering that of late we had neglected our Scientific Note Book, for twenty-four hours we collected statistics on the motion picture industry, and very attractive figures they were!

XXIX

Escape from Lindbergh Field

BY SUNDAY NOON our tank was once more repaired.
Down the coast we flew to reach the lower mountains of
the coastal range before heading east. With a thick fog
a short distance off the coast and a general fog above 1000
feet, we had to fly low along the shore. At Lindbergh Field,
San Diego, we stopped for lunch and gas. Our Massachusetts
registration attracted some attention.

"Where's your N. C.?" we were asked.

In the morning paper we had read how the French fliers,
Dieudonné Costa and Maurice Bellonte, were just starting
on their good will tour encircling the United States after
their successful flight from Paris. If they could, why could
not we?

Up we spoke; "This is a good will flight around the
country. We are spreading good will from Massachusetts.
You wouldn't stop us, would you?"

Then we saw attractive Ruth Alexander and her red
monoplane in which she had just broken the record for
a non-stop flight from Canada to Mexico. In two days she
was to attempt a record flight to New York. "I'll see you
in Wichita," she smiled, climbing into her cockpit for a test
hop.

"Afraid we can't wait," we laughed back, little realizing
the prophetic significance of our words.

Quite a crowd of Sunday onlookers had gathered to inspect
our small plane from Massachusetts. The man who sold
us gas still seemed disturbed by our lack of a Federal license.
"Why, there are only three states in the United States where
you're allowed to fly without a Federal license." He named

the three, among them Arizona. "If you're going to Los Angles, you'll never get away with it."

"We're not going," we protested, "we just came from there. But what would they do to us anyhow?"

"If a state inspector caught you, he'd ground you for at least a week."

By this time I was in the cockpit and Pete had just turned her over. One turn was enough. As Pete walked around the wing, I noticed a man in the smart uniform of a state inspector walking rapidly toward us from the hangar.

I motioned Pete to hurry. "For gosh sake, get in," I called. "I don't like his looks."

Pete realized the situation, and tossing his parachute in the front cockpit without bothering to put it on, he quickly climbed in on top of it. Flit was headed cross-wind across the field. As politely as our time permitted, we asked the onlookers to step back. Pete called "Arizona next," I gave Flit the gun and before the nonplussed state inspector knew what it was all about, we had made a cross-wind take-off from the famous Lindbergh Field.

"Thank God we're out of that state," came through the ear phones as we climbed above the city.

"We're not out yet." After climbing to 2000 feet, we headed east above the haze for the San Jacinto Mountains. So began the last leg of our journey, the long flight across the continent.

XXX

Arizona Revisited

IN THE WINTER OF 1917 I had motored in a small Dodge car east from San Diego over the mountains into Imperial Valley, down the valley into Yuma where California and Arizona touch Mexico, thence across the Arizona desert into Phoenix. It is always interesting to see again from other angles and after the passage of time, places we have seen before, so I was thrilled to see that our course followed closely the road I had traversed over thirteen years earlier.

I remember how in those days it was a long, slow climb up the coastal range, and how in the higher altitudes although we were at 7000 feet and the month was February, frequent stops for water were necessary to cool the overheated engine. I remember that after hours of winding through the mountains, we started down the eastern slopes, and never had I seen more barren, lonely, rocky country. Then coasting down the steep and scary mountain road, we approached the fertile Imperial Valley, simply the former desert reclaimed to life by irrigation.

The first night after a long day of travel, I recall, we had stopped at the little town of El Centro, near the Mexican border and a very good day's run we had made, or so I thought. Yes, and I remember at the hotel that evening I bought a copy of the *The Winning of Barbara Worth* by Harold Bell Wright and read all about the country we were then exploring.

But it was the next day when we crossed the desert southeast of the Salton Sea that we really did our pioneering. For sixty miles we saw no sign of a town. The one road consisted of ruts made by the previous car across the desert and in case the wind had blown these over, wooden poles erected every half mile were the only guide to direct us. It was long before the days of balloon tires and we had let most of the air out of our tires to get a wider surface which would keep the car from sinking into the sand. Fords and Dodges were the only practical cars for such a trip, and a Dodge was almost too heavy. At first the dry soil supported cactus and mesquite bushes but eventually these thinned out and we came upon fine desert sand. A narrow plank road had been constructed for six miles across the dunes and at the end of this plank road there was a filling station. It was a long, hot morning's ride and on reaching Yuma for lunch, the thermometer read 105 degrees in the shade. I recall how impressed I was to see Indians with their leather-like feet walking barefoot on the hot tar pavements. That night we stopped at Palomas on the Gila River, a well-defined town on the map, but in real life a general store with two rooms for travellers. As the travellers' rooms were taken, we slept on the porch and battled scorpions.

This trip represented two days of steady driving in a Dodge and on the third day we reached Phoenix feeling like true western pioneers. But that was thirteen and a half years ago, back in February 1917.

Across this same country Pete and I now headed on our dash east. It was after 2:30 p.m. when we had staged our hasty getaway from Lindbergh Field. Half an hour later we were above the barren, rocky mountains and reservoirs which lay on either side of the course we had plotted. A short distance beyond as the mountains fell away, we could look north and see the alkali Salton Sea sparkling in the sunlight and before entering the Imperial Valley we passed directly over a smaller alkali lake. For old times' sake, I waved to El Centro and thought of Barbara Worth, but although it was only an hour and a half since we had left San Diego, we could not take the time to stop. Even from the air the town seemed larger than I remembered it.

Across the sixty miles of desert we set Flit's nose. There were the same cactus and mesquite bushes, warning us not to land. As we neared the fine sand with the rolling dunes, we spotted the same plank road to assure us we were on our course. The planks were now almost covered by sand

and a short distance away was a fine cement road cutting a straight line across the trackless waste. Thirteen years showed changes even in the desert.

We stopped at Yuma long enough to refuel and were off again to make the best of daylight hours. Beyond Yuma we circled over Mexico so we could say we had been there and then followed the dry bed of the Gila River east. The country continued much the same, slightly rolling, covered with cactus and mesquite, but still barren enough to be called desert. Seventy miles out of Yuma we passed over the town of Palomas, which still consisted of a solitary building, and thirty miles beyond we landed at the town of Gila Bend, so-called on account of the sharp bend in the river at this point where it turns northward into Phoenix. In four hours that afternoon we had crossed mountains and deserts which had taken me two days and a half to cross by automobile in 1917, and then we thought that we had made a rapid trip. It is over such country as this that an aeroplane really does save time.

We could have made Phoenix before dark, but from Gila Bend we had decided to head southeast and cut across the Papago Indian Reservation into Tucson, thereby saving some fifty miles of distance. To be sure, the country would be wild and barren, but so was that which we had already traversed; moreover, this was Monday night and on the morrow we were due in Boston.

I have recently read Lieutenant Tomlinson's exciting book, *The Sky's the Limit*. In that he has described landing at Gila Bend back in 1921 during a flight across the country in an old "Jenny." On stopping there again in 1922, he again found old tins cans littering up the field. He described slipping into the field across the railroad tracks and past the gas tanks. Yes, Lieutenant, we saw the same tin cans scattered about and after bouncing a little at the far end of the uneven field we rolled to a stop beside the framework of a rusty old bed; and in the bushes beyond was the wreck of an automobile, or was it the fuselage of a forsaken plane?

We taxied back toward the houses at the southern end of the field while half the town strolled out to meet us.

"Where can we get gas?" we asked one of the advance guard.

"Down the road at the Standard Oil tank."

The Standard Oil tank and several others were a short distance down the main road, almost in the center of town. The field was exposed to winds, and we thought that behind one of these tanks there would be a nice sheltered spot for Flit to spend the night. But the dust kicked up by our propeller on the dry ground was terrific.

"Is it all right to taxi down to the tank?" we inquired hesitantly.

"You're in Arizona now. Do what you please."

"But won't the people mind the dust?"

"The hell with 'em. Don't ask."

And off the field, onto the road, and down the main street of Gila Bend went Flit, still followed by the townsfolk bathed in dust.

The hotel was clean, and our room opened on a sleeping porch one story above the main street. As the night was warm and clear, it did not take us long to move our mattresses out on the porch, where we slept soundly below the brilliant Arizona stars.

The oil man was up early to give us gas. Again we taxied down the street as the sharp reports of the exhaust informed all would-be sleepers that Flit was on her way. Why should anyone want to sleep on such a clear, beautiful morning? At two houses beside the field we could see people on the porches still in bed. Fortunately, there was no wind so that we headed Flit where we wished and did not cover them with dust in taking off. My last recollection of the town was peeking out of the corner of my eye, just as we left the ground and seeing a man on the nearest porch jump out of bed and quickly pull on his pants.

Tucson, Lordsburg and El Paso. Somehow they do not sound far apart nor do they appear so on the airline time table, but between those cities there is a lot of wild and barren country. Even now this flight seems blurred; there was such a sameness to it—flat unfertile country with cactus and mesquite, then miles of gradually rising table land, barren mountains of a peculiar red and purple shade, rugged valleys and gorges, then more dry river bottoms and desert land. In the midday heat we saw wind twisters like little water spouts of sand cutting their way across the dusty ground. Once near Deming we counted thirty at one time. They never bothered us, except for an occasional little bump, but we wondered if they ever combined into one big twister. If so, we did not wish to be around. This is the country for terrific thunderstorms which come up rapidly and make flying very dangerous, so we watched the clouds carefully. Having to spend all our daylight hours in the air had put our nerves on edge and the realization that we had flown so far without mishap magnified possible dangers that might yet come. The Army Lieutenant at Lordsburg said the season for thunderstorms was about over so our chances of missing them were good. This was encouraging. The Weather Bureau at San Diego had told us that conditions never looked better for a flight across the continent than on the day we left. At that time they were having terrific downpours in the Mississippi Valley but these would all be over before we reached the central states. Perhaps our luck would see us through after all.

At Tucson we stopped at the Municipal Field and met a Mr. Mays who knew flying friends of ours in Boston. Ever since leaving Seattle, we had tried to obtain United States Government strip maps for our flight East, but in our experience Washington and Boston were the only places where we found these maps available. Mr. Mays knew the country well and had just come through from Wichita, Kansas.

As he had come over the route we wished to follow, we asked him to direct us. The way from Tucson to El Paso looked easy on the Rand McNally map, but from El Paso to Roswell, it was a mystery. Unfortunately, Texas is such a large state that the publishers have found it necessary to cut off the extreme edges of the state and insert them here and there in unused corners of the map. In following a course which happens to traverse one of these misplaced edges of the state, it is rather difficult to get one's bearings with the rest of the state.

In the hot sun before the hangar, Mr. Mays knelt and

traced out on the smooth sand surface of the field his own map of the country from El Paso to Roswell. I made a copy of it and notes of his directions.

A peculiar buzzing noise interrupted us. I looked up and just inside the hangar door not six feet from where we were standing were two huge rattle snakes, coiled and ready to spring. At first I did not notice that they were in a large, glass case with a wire netting at the top to protect us from their deadly fangs! Upon further investigation, we were interested to find the pilots at Tucson had, as additional pets, a moccasin snake and several Gila monsters, all of which had been captured on the field. Ordinarily, one does not include snakes among the flying hazards but, had we spent the night at Tucson, we should have wanted to look in the cockpit in the morning to make sure rattlers had not crawled in before us.

Mr. Mays' map seemed clear and quite simple, and we left Tucson much cheered about the route east of El Paso, which heretofore had caused us some anxiety.

XXXI

Lost

"LANDED AT STANDARD FIELD, El Paso, after rough old trip, 3:30 p.m."

So reads our log. The wind twisters and the heat waves over the mountains caused the roughness. For the last few miles before reaching El Paso we had followed the dashing Rio Grande where it flows down from the northwest and skirts the western edge of the Orange Mountains. At the city we had turned sharply to the east through the deep gap where the river had eaten at the mountain for centuries. Flying through this huge cut and out across the city gave me the feeling of passing through a continental gateway dividing west from east. The several large airports at El Paso were all located in a general northeasterly direction from the city. We selected the field of the Western Air Express as one where we could most likely obtain information for the balance of the journey. But, alas, still no strip maps! So we resorted to our copy of Mr. Mays' sand map and the following notes we had scribbled as he talked:

"Leave the Hueco Mountains well on your left and go south of the Sacramento Mountains. They are only about 10,000 feet high, and you can go over them straight to Roswell, but it is better country if you go south of the Sacramento Mountains and then north between them and the next range. As you round the Sacramento Mountains, you will not think there is any way through, because they appear to overlap the next range, but follow up the eastern side of the Sacramento range and your course will open up. Soon after leaving El Paso, before reaching the mountains, you will pick up a strong tail wind that will blow you all the way to Roswell. I've never failed to find it. Three

120

thousand feet above the ground you'll find a thirty-mile breeze."

As a strong tail wind would be the prevailing wind, this sounded reasonable enough. From the Western Air Express officials we received cordial treatment and the latest weather reports which promised good conditions to the eastward.

At 4:00 sharp we took off for Roswell, about 160 miles distant and laid our course to pass between the mountains. Soon after leaving El Paso and as we neared the Hueco Mountains, we noticed a strange blue haze in the atmosphere. It seemed to be a heat wave rising from the desert and was thickest near the mountains, almost concealing them at close range. After passing the Hueco Mountains, we saw the bare outlines of more mountains to the north, but in the haze we could not tell their distance. Mindful of the danger of mountain flying in a fog, we bore further south to what we thought must be the Sacramento range. The country underneath was flat. Cactus and scrub growth were still the only vegetation and we had seen no sign of habitation since leaving El Paso. We had been heading slightly north of east, but had not yet flown far enough to clear the southern edge of the Sacramento Mountains. We thought they must be the dark outline ahead which loomed across the plains. Or were those the Guadaloupe Mountains which stretched to the southward of the Sacramento range? Here and there were possible landings where we might put down—flat plains without a sign of life or vegetation. God spare us from landing in such lonely country! Near the Hueco Mountains we had noticed several small lakes, but for miles since then we had seen no sign of water.

There was one shining spot which looked like the dry bed of a salt lake, but there was no water.

We soon passed a small water hole, a sort of puddle in the desert. I wrote down the time of passing and tried to identify the location for possible future use. In case we were forced down, our two ginger ale bottles containing water could not last long.

It seemed like hours after passing this first water hole that we continued over the same dry flat plains. In reality it was only about half an hour. But it was long enough to impress us with a greater feeling of loneliness than anything we had experienced before. We saw a few more water holes and I noted them all. Now the land was rising and to the north the mountains showed clearly. We had crossed two dry river valleys and had run our allotted distance east to pass the Sacramento Mountains, but saw no sign of the promised opening between the ranges. We realized at last that we were definitely lost. There was nothing left to do but carry on across the mountains which loomed threateningly ahead. The haze seemed to evaporate in the late afternoon, and the atmosphere suddenly become clearer.

We were already flying at 6000 feet and we now turned Flit's nose towards one saddle-back between two higher knobs, and climbed. We were only 1500 feet above the ground, and could distinguish a well defined Indian trail winding back and forth to the top of this saddle-back. At 6500 feet we were level with the pass, so we circled and climbed another 1000 feet before venturing through. Flying low above these mountains was dangerous, but it was getting late and we had no time to spare. The strong tail winds we had been promised had not materialized. All the way across the plains from El Paso head winds had held us back, and now as we climbed up this pass, they gave us a real struggle. Shades of the Rockies passed through my mind. When at last we literally dove through the pass, the winds lightened and favored. Miles of rugged canyon country opened in a great panorama before us but with no sign of civilization or ground on which to land. With less than one hour before darkness, our future was not propitious. Yes, we were lost. Somewhere ahead we knew there was the Pecos River and a railroad track running north and south. It might be thirty miles or it might be a hundred. That all depended where we were. Once on that track we could follow north until we found a town, assuming that both daylight and our supply of gasoline held out. If not, well, we should have to land even though this was not the kind of country which ordinarily inspired such ideas. In any case, this was our only hope; so we headed east for the river and the railroad tracks and opened up our motor.

On its eastern slopes this mountain range was cut with deep canyon-like valleys and through these valleys prospectors' trails wound precipitously. In our efforts to make every second count we were low enough, if not to enjoy, at least to notice the details below. I wondered if we came down in that canyon and "squashed" in safely at the bottom, which trail would lead us to food and water; and if we reached that ridge, then which way should we head? Lost? Yes, completely, and what a country to have chosen! But we were not the first flyers to get lost in strange mountains and we had not yet crashed into a mountain side; Flit was still performing perfectly. We could see that the territory ahead was gradually flattening out into deep, dry river bottoms. There we might find room to put down. If we kept our heads, we could get out of this fix yet. Do it ourselves we must, for we alone could safely land the plane and no one knew our whereabouts to send us help.

Behind us the sun still promised over half an hour of daylight. The tank still showed a quarter full, and that would last till dark. Ahead the river valleys were concentrating, tributaries of the greater stream, and leaving more flat country in the valleys. During this time Pete and I conversed occasionally, just for encouragement. Pete knew the sun and gas were getting low but he realized that it was just as important as either gas or sun not to let our spirits fall too low.

"I think next year I'll go to Europe for the summer."

"So do I. On a boat, you mean."

"Yes. Say the Europa."

"What's that ahead?"

"What?"

"That tank!"

"My gosh! Looks like a water tower."

What a relief! We knew not what it was but it was something made by human hands, though still several miles ahead. To gain better speed we were flying less than 500 feet above the ground and this tank-like object rose distinctly against the sky line. For over an hour we had not seen the slightest semblance of a place where we could safely land a plane and, although a water tower on the horizon was hardly a landing field, it cheered us up a lot. As we neared the tower, there below us appeared a narrow clearing in the brush. We dove and passed low over it.

"Pete, we could get in there."

"Sure, we could, or make a darn good try."

Around the water tower were four houses with neat little gardens and on the porch of each house were people waving violently as we flew over. We circled twice very low and pointed back toward the clearing we had passed. Apparently they saw us point for several men jumped in a waiting Ford and started down a narrow trail in the direction we had pointed.

With thumping hearts we headed back for our prospective landing field. The sun had just dipped below the horizon. There was the clearing, white and chalky amidst the dusty, brown bushes. Once more we glided over a few feet above the ground, to get a better view. It had the appearance of a small lake bottom where a deposit of alkali or salt had killed the foliage, which was only just beginning to grow again. The ground looked hard, almost claylike, and fairly smooth except for occasional stubble and small cactus. The entire clearing was just a narrow strip hemmed in with cactus and mesquite bushes four to six feet high.

As there was very little wind, we decided to come in the long way of the field but, without any wind to hold us back, we wondered whether Flit would stop before striking the bushes at the far end of the field. This was our problem. Except for a few scattered bushes the field was wide enough, and I felt sure we could slip in between the bushes. If Flit would only stop! Too bad we had no brakes on her. In any case, the field was a Godsend, for here at least we could get *ourselves* down safely.

As we circled, I realized this landing was looming as the real test of our trip. If we were to come through a crisis, this was our chance to show it. The slightest miscalculation would mean the end of Flit and leave us many days from home with our vacation at an end.

Again we circled back; then with a gentle glide we came in. Flit did her stuff. We cleared the bushes at the near edge of the field by inches, slipped sharply between two Spanish dagger plants till our wing almost scraped the earth, flattened out quickly, felt solid ground beneath our tail skid, and Flit, with the propeller kicking over slowly, rolled to a stop between two cactus stalks.

XXXII

Blodgett Field, Orla

PETE TURNED AROUND and smiled, and I smiled back. There was not much to say, but we were both glad God had seen fit to place an airport there. I called it Blodgett Field. Pete had never had an airport named for him before.

We dismounted and pulled Flit into the lee of the largest mesquite bush, to which we tied her for the night. This act was interrupted by the arrival of two Fords, which came winding through the bushes bearing a reception committee of six men. They seemed as glad to see us as we were to see them and no doubt equally surprised.

"I've lived here for three years and this is the first time I knew there was a place around here big enough to land an airplane," volunteered one of them.

Assured that cattle and jackrabbits would be Flit's only molesters during the night, we quickly secured the engine and cockpit covers and were soon bouncing through the bushes to the Standard Oil of California Pipe Line Pumping Station at Orla, Texas. It was fifty-five miles from the nearest town, and we were about 100 miles south of Roswell, our destination.

By going too far south of the Sacramento Range, we had failed to find the opening on its eastern slope and had strayed 100 miles from our course. Twelve miles further on they said, we should have struck the Pecos River and on the far bank of this river was the railroad track running north and south. But there was no town there and before reaching civilization, we should have had to follow the tracks about fifty miles north to the famous cave town of Carlsbad.

TO ALASKA AND BACK

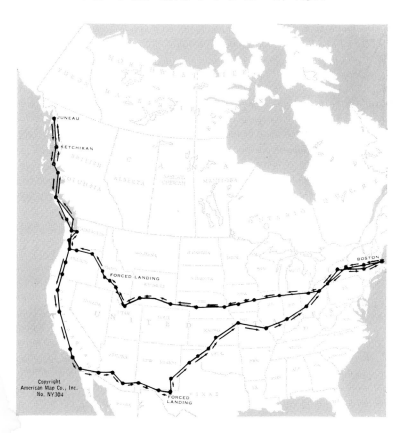

Transcontinental Flying in 1930 Had its Ups and Downs.
Each Star Indicates a Landing, Not All of Them Planned.

Flit's Far Landing Places: Parco, Wyoming, 7800 feet high . . .

refueling Flit at a gasoline station in Ketchikan . . .

and an unexpected, but welcome, stop at Blodgett Field.

Since flying over this country, I have read the thrilling story of *Six Years with the Texas Rangers* by J. B. Gillett and was particularly interested in his description of the lands east of El Paso. These were the last stamping grounds of the hostile Apache Indians around 1880, where the dangers from both Indians and lack of water were well recogized by the Rangers.

In January 1880 two mining engineers appeared at the Rangers' camp in Ysleta, near El Paso bound for Roswell, New Mexico. The men proposed to follow "the old abandoned Butterfield stage route, which leads by Hueco Tanks, Alamo Springs, Cornidas Mountain, Crow Flat and Guadalup Mountain, and thence to the Pecos River."

Mr. Gillett tells how Lieutenant Baylor warned the men "that this was a very dangerous route, without a living white man from Ysleta to the Pecos River, more than 150 miles distant, and through an Indian country all the way." It is interesting to note that this is exactly the course we followed. Somehow knowing that the points along the way have names and have been ranged over before makes a course seem a little less hazardous, but his description is not very reassuring.

South of the salt lakes which we had seen at the foot of the Guadalupe Mountains, Mr. Gillett describes one route where for a distance of ninety miles there was not a drop of water on the way. After being ambushed by the Indians and losing all their horses, the two mining engineers, although experienced campers, finally returned to the Rangers' camp more dead than alive from their tramp over the rough, arid country.

There were no Indians when we flew over, but neither were there any white men to take their places and give us water. I think it is just as well that we did not put down.

We certainly had been lucky to find an opportunity to land and refuel. Our next problem was how to get out of Blodgett Field, but this could wait until the morrow. Besides, we could not forget the object of our trip. There was much of scientific value to be learned at a Pipe Line Pumping Station, and it was already getting dark.

As we drove into the settlement we were met by Mr.

McAnarney, the superintendent, and the balance of the seventeen inhabitants at the station. Although the boys had offered us the hospitality of the bunk house, Mr. "Mac" insisted on our staying at his more palatial shack. Mrs. Doherty, cook for the station, prepared a late supper, and our worries of the afternoon were soon forgotten in hearing stories about the interesting, if lonely, life at a West Texas pumping station.

This station was on the pipe line running to El Paso. Fifty miles to the east a similar station at Wink pumped the oil to this station at Orla, and here three fine-looking turbines took up the burden and pushed the oil another thirty-one miles to the next station at Guadaloupe.

After a delicious repast of ham and eggs, Mr. "Mac" took us on a tour of inspection about the plant. We were greatly impressed with its neatness and business-like appearance. To us, one of the most interesting points was a large water basin 200 feet square and containing four feet of water. Although constructed primarily for fire protection, in hot weather it served as a swimming pool and must have been a great relief to the members of the plant.

Officials of the Standard Oil Company had already talked of clearing away space behind the houses for a landing field to afford rapid transportation between stations so, although ours was the only plane to have landed at Orla, Texas, probably not for long shall we hold that distinction and is it even doubtful if Blodgett Field will be selected as the exact site of the airport.

"Never mind, Pete, not all flyers have a field named for them, even for a short time."

Pete's ardor for statistics about pumping stations outlasted mine. The sight of a bed decided me and somehow I felt it not unreasonable to call it a day. What luck it was to have that big double bed on which to rest our weary frames, out there in the wilds of Texas.

"I'm due at the office tomorrow," said Pete as he rolled over taking all the sheet.

"So am I. But we're a lot nearer home than we were four hours ago," I replied. It was a hot night; he could have the sheet.

XXXIII

Bigger and Better Airports

SEPTEMBER 16. Up at 6:00 a.m., before the sun. Mrs. "Mac" had eggs and coffee for us. Out to plane with five gallons of automobile gas. Took off at 8:00 a.m. for Carlsbad. Landed Roswell 9:30.

In our brief log there was no space to record how we spent the time between 7:00 and 8:00 breaking down the rugged cactus and Spanish dagger plants to give us a sufficiently long runway from which to take off; nor how we taxied the plane up to the very end of the clearing and gave her the gun once for a short run to see how quickly we could gain speed and to estimate our chances of getting off Blodgett Field.

Our estimate was good. We held Flit's tail high and her nose down until the last minute—thus getting all possible speed—pulled the stick back quickly and Flit leaped into the air. We cleared the bushes by feet and left Blodgett Field as handily as we had come.

As we flew up the Pecos River, we were doubly thankful to have seen the water tank at Orla and to have decided to land. The railroad tracks now seemed to offer the only landing field as we continued north towards Carlsbad, although I have never considered railroad tracks entirely adequate for this purpose.

From Orla to Roswell, a distance of about 100 miles, we followed the Pecos River north, passing over the Carlsbad caves about midway between the towns.

As we looked down from 1000 feet for some sign of the entrance, Pete called through the voice tube, "I'm glad to have seen the Carlsbad caves."

After our southern detour, it was a relief to realize that

from Roswell east we would be following an established air line with emergency landing fields every hour or so and an occasional plane to wave to in the distance.

A mail pilot at Roswell field told us to be sure to follow the pipe line to Wichita, as it was much the simplest way to keep on our course. For some time we scanned the ground below in vain for the pipe line, but finally we detected a light brown streak cutting straight across the countryside. At times it was faint and almost indistinct, but soon our eyes became accustomed to the little brown line which avoided towns, forded rivers and lead us on a course straighter than roads or railroad tracks.

From Roswell to Boston, our flight, to me, is practically a blurred recollection of landings and take-offs. We were anxious to reach Boston as soon as possible and we had mapped out a schedule of daily flights. Each day was a race to maintain our schedule. Each landing we checked off with keen satisfaction and each night we congratulated each other upon arriving one day nearer our goal. In the minds of both there persisted a wonder as to whether we could actually accomplish the entire trip without a mishap. With this wonder a strange tenseness crept in and we felt that we had to be increasingly careful not to take any foolish chances. We were like the winning team at sport which starts by playing safe and often suffers as a result. But in our case I think this extra caution served to offset any over-confidence which we might have felt as the country became more favorable to flying and the landing fields more frequent.

Some flights, some landing fields and certain incidents stand out more clearly than others, but in general our four days from Orla to Boston are a confused memory.

English Field at Amarillo, Texas, in the center of the so-called Texas Panhandle, had been described to us as one of the best in the country. Although it was a large, flat field, just one mile square, to us it lacked character and attraction. Possibly it was the bumpy air above the Panhandle which caused our unfavorable reaction; or possibly it was the sight of the poor seasick passengers who dragged themselves out of the large Fokker transport plane as we stepped into the

Two Greater Boston Fliers Descend Safely in Alaska

Lombard of Winchester and Blodgett of New- Plan Big Game Hunt in the Mountains

Two Bear-Killing Flyers Are Back From Northland

n Boston across the
British Columbia,
ird of Winchester,

stages, depending largely on maps to
guide their way across British Columbia
and then fly along the coast to Alaska.

Boston—the city
brains—has its migh
Two of them are
bard, attorney, and 1
ett, banker, wno fl
meet some bears a
ing home again w!
Each man shot
took pictures of m
bard bagged a sil
Admiralty Island
ing after six b

BOSTON MEN HOP TO ALASKA, BAG 2 BEARS IN 14 DAYS

to Al
and 1

END VACATION TRIP BY PLANE

HOME AFTER 11,000-MILE FLIGHT

THE BOSTON HERALD, SAT

PAIR JOYOUS OVER VACATION, FLYING TO ALASKA IN PLANE

Boston Men Take Outing by Journeying Across Country and Going
North to Enjoy Hunting and Fishing.

Two young men from Boston, who dropped in at S
terday after flight across continent on their wa
shown standing in front of the light plane. Fron
N. Lombard and Frederick N. Blodgett.
FIVE forced landings on the 2000-
mile flight from Boston, the dan-

with pontoon
continue to A
gers in dodging electric storms to land in lat

BOSTON SUNDAY POST SECOND COLOR-FEATURE SECTION, MARCH 13, 1932

Charged by a Giant Bear
---And These Boston Hunters Flew 12,000 Miles to Get Thrill of Their Lives

Fred Blodgett and Lawrence Lombard
Tell of a Record Nimrod Jaunt to
Alaska in Rickety Airplane to Tackle
Mighty Kodiak Bruins and Back
Again Within a Month

Once They Thought Plane
Was Falling to Pieces—
Another Time They Had
to Take Off on Main Street

By John P. Cuppswell

In 1930, A Flight Like Flit's Was Major News Across the Country

office; but I suspect the principal reason was the fact that everyone at English Field seemed over-anxious to tell us how wonderful it was. We might have liked it better had we been given a chance to praise the field to them. We could stand modest pride, but this noisy concert was too much!

Our schedule called for Wichita that night. We might have gone a few miles further but Pete had friends at Wichita. The pipe line led us over gently rolling farm country, still wet and fresh from recent rains, straight to the famous "Air City."

Our map showed airports at the southeast corner of the city but, long before we reached the city itself, we could see numerous airports ahead, with frequent planes rising above the trees and houses as they took off or disappearing behind them as they landed. After circling a bit, we found the Municipal Field with the Stearman factory at one side. The field was a rich green and looked more like a huge golf course than an airport. As we glided down to our landing, we saw the terrain was gently rolling, but the grass was so smooth and soft that it seemed a bad landing would be impossible. It reminded me of how much easier it is to hit a golf ball from a smooth, well-kept tee than from a rough, shabby one.

"This is the finest airport we've seen yet," we volunteered to Pete's classmate, Fred Doyle, who met us at the hangar.

"Yes, Lindbergh says it's the best airport in the country," Fred replied with pride.

"What does Lindbergh know about it?" I asked. "When he flies across the country he only lands about twice, but we've landed in practically every back yard and open field in America and when *we* tell you this is the best, that's a real compliment."

The brother of Pete's friend had flown to Kansas City on business that morning and was due back on the afternoon plane. As we walked to the other end of the hangar, we heard the drone of the transport plane and in came the big Fokker, landed and taxied up to the steps at the end of the canopy-covered walk. The passengers alighted with no more excitement or bustle than if they were getting off a subway train. As the plane had been full, the "brother" was due on the next section, and in five minutes with the same smoothness and efficiency in came another Fokker and out stepped the "brother."

I wish Pete had not always made our take-offs so difficult. His friends the Doyles, both Dartmouth graduates, and their very hospitable parents urged us to stay over, at least a week. The duck season had opened the day before, and the yarns we were told about duck shooting on the Mississippi were almost more than we could resist. Just one morning was all we needed. If only we could have dispensed with our New England consciences! But we were to fly back next year to check up on the stories.

Our visit at Wichita was saddened by reading at breakfast of the tragic death of Ruth Alexander after taking off from Lindbergh Field. Apparently she had found difficulty in gaining altitude with her heavily laden plane and, in the morning fog which so frequently hangs over the coast line, she had crashed into a high hill behind the field. It was at Wichita that she had promised to wave to us.

We could not help thinking of the hazy mountains in New Mexico over which we had been lost and of our fortunate landing at Orla. Of course, our plane being slower than Miss Alexander's, had the added safeguard of a slower landing speed, but even this could not eliminate the danger of fog, and we resolved again to be doubly careful for the remainder of our trip.

XXXIV

A Cool Reception

THE PRESENT MOTH FACTORY is at St. Louis and we had wired ahead to it to have two new gas tanks ready for immediate installation. Since we left Los Angeles the center section tank, our only remaining one, had given us more worry than actual trouble. We knew it was only a question of time, however, before it would begin to leak again, with the attendant delay of having to have it soldered.

After our successful flight to Alaska, we fully expected the Moth Company to receive us with open arms, and the least we expected were new gas tanks to replace our troublesome ones. We even wondered if they would not want Flit for advertising purposes, or for the Smithsonian Institute to place beside Colonel Lindbergh's "Spirit of St. Louis," but in this case we were going to insist on flying back to Boston before exchanging Flit for a new Moth.

At 3:20 Wednesday afternoon we landed at Lambert Field, St. Louis, from which Colonel Lindbergh had flown to New York for his trans-Atlantic flight. We came down near the Curtis Robertson hangar where a number of Moths were drawn up on the line. The next hour was spent interviewing one minor official of the Curtis Company after another. By 5 o'clock I had succeeded in locating a man who knew that we had wired ahead for gas tanks, but he informed us it was too late to do anything that night. "It's too bad your tank leaks. All the old ones leak. We are using a better type now." Small consolation, this, to Pete and me.

We were furious! What a reception from the Moth Company! We longed for Jump Goodwin of the Alaska Washington Airways in Seattle, who had never worked on a Moth

until he saw ours. He would have had the tanks installed
that night and Flit checked over and ready to take off at
dawn.

When Pete and I learned that Moths were no longer being
built and that ships like Flit which had cost $5,000 within
the year, were being sold new at St. Louis for $3,000, we
began to understand. The depression had already hit the
aviation industry and private planes were rapidly becoming
a drug on the market.

At St. Louis my college pride received another blow. One
of my best friends, Chet Wright, who had been a leading
Ace in World War I, lived in St. Louis. Having recently
experienced St. Louis hospitality as an usher in Chet's wed-
ding to Margaret Caradine, I wired him to get out the band.
For days I had been promising Pete a change from Dartmouth hospitality. But now after being told a new gas tank
could not be installed until the following forenoon, I found
that Chet was out of town. Somewhat daunted, I transferred
my efforts to a good Yale friend, Ethan Shepley, and even
Harvard could not have surpassed the hospitality which we
were shown.

It was afternoon on Thursday before we got away from
Lambert Field with one new gas tank and a new temperature gauge. Cleveland by night was our objective. Cleveland
was the first place we had visited on our flight west and we
had promised to stop on our return to show my sister we
were still alive.

We laid the straightest possible course from St. Louis to
Cleveland, abandoning the air lines and simply stopping at
those airports nearest our line of flight. Our first stop was
at Terre Haute where we had lunch. The young lady behind
the counter told us flying there had received a severe set-
back a couple of weeks previous. The two most popular
amateur pilots at the field had collided when having a little
fun in the air.

Flying is still sufficiently in its infancy so that deaths
from flying accidents are featured in the press and stand out
in one's memory. I have enumerated the accidents which
came particularly to our attention on the trip. Actually we
heard of surprisingly few serious ones considering the amount

of time we spent around airports talking with the flying fraternity. As aviation increases, probably flying accidents will attract no more attention than motor accidents do today. Already the Department of Commerce statistics show that the proportion of accidents to the miles flown has decreased tremendously during the last few years.

Troy, Ohio, is the next town to stand out in my mind, as here we wasted fifteen minutes circling the countryside in a vain search for a landing field. We had seen the field at the Waco plant on the south side of the river, but our Rand McNally map showed another airport across the river. Thinking this must be the municipal field, we continued on. Fortunately, the result was no more serious than a loss of time and at last we turned back across the river and landed where the well-known Waco planes are made. They were glad to supply a Moth with gasoline and oil. The other airport existed only on the map, we were informed.

Although we knew the field, having landed there on our way west, our landing on the outskirts of Cleveland almost ended in disaster. Darkness was falling fast when we arrived above the little airport. We had circled several times above the neighborhood where my sister lives to warn her of our approach so she could motor to the field to meet us.

The field is long and narrow, running in a northerly and southerly direction. There was almost no wind as we came in from the south headed toward the hangar at the northern end of the field. I remembered a ditch which crossed the field at right angles near the southern edge. Pete remembered it too and warned me not to let our wheels touch until we had cleared the ditch. There was plenty of room beyond for a proper landing. We glided low over the ditch. Slowly pulling the stick all the way back, I waited for Flit to settle, but instead she continued to drift. I felt quickly for the stabilizer, but it was back in proper position for landing. Still we floated three feet above the ground without apparent loss of speed. The hangar loomed rapidly on our left. When near the ground it is impossible to see directly in front of the plane, but ahead at the end of the field, I could see a rough section, then a road with tall trees beyond. It was too late to take to the air again. Finally our wheels touched the ground, but we were still travelling too fast to stop within the limits of the field. As we passed, I noticed two automobiles and several people standing in front of the hangar. We bounced over the road on to the rough ground beyond. The trees and a large post were coming fast. At such times one is supposed to relive one's entire past, but all I could think of was how lucky it was that those people and the automobiles had stopped near the hangar, as they might just as well have been directly in our course. There was no chance of stopping. Could we make a turn at this speed? I pushed the right foot pedal and shoved the stick hard left. Flit turned sharply to the right in a ground loop, tipped a little, and with a final bounce came to a halt.

"Another safe landing!" I called to Pete.

"You said it. Thank God we've only one more day," he answered.

I climbed out sheepishly to be greeted by my sister and three nephews who had been interested spectators of the worst landing of our entire trip. This was bad enough but how much worse would it have been had Flit found her final resting place against their waiting motor car and Pete and I had been forced to take the train for the last 700 miles of our journey.

Our landing at Cleveland certainly did not serve to lessen the tension of our last day's flight, tension not so much from fear of danger, but fear lest after having come so far some small accident might mar the completion of our trip. To date our Gipsy motor had performed valiantly. For days we had been wondering whether it could hold without more than the occasional checks it had been receiving. Ten thousand miles is a long distance for a motor without a pretty thorough examination.

When we arrived at Omaha on our trip west, in order to save weight, we had left all the maps which we had used to that point, expecting to pick them up on our return. When changing our route we had wired for the maps to be forwarded to Cleveland. They had not arrived, so we were without maps from Cleveland to Boston. The route is not difficult to find, however, and as I had thrice before flown over this country, I had a pretty good idea of where the airports were. Rochester and Albany were our only stops for fuel. It was a clear day with a favorable wind and we flew high to get all the benefit possible from the stronger breeze aloft.

XXXV

Home

THE FLIGHT FROM ALBANY to Boston is always beautiful on a clear day and the familiar landmarks looked particularly welcome to us on this occasion. Soon after leaving the Berkshires, we began to see the reflection of the sun on the Atlantic Ocean ahead. Mt. Wachusett looked small in comparison with the western mountains we had seen and, as we passed over it, we could see the Customs House tower at Boston, although still fifty miles away.

All the way from Mt. Wachusett we were gradually losing altitude and with her nose down Flit was racing home at ninety-five miles an hour. Over the Charles River Basin we throttled the motor and came down in a steep glide towards the familiar airport. It was a welcome sight. We circled Skyways and the East Coast hangars and waved and to our surprise men came running out and waved back. Ordinarily one lone mechanic might look up and wave. The snappy thing to do would be to slip down smartly close to Flit's stall in the Skyways hangar, but we were taking no chances with our last landing and came down gently in the middle of the airport and taxied toward our hangar. To our amazement we were met by news photographers asking us to stop before dismounting.

"Where have you been?" they queried. "We expected you on Wednesday."

"Where are your bear skins?" another shouted.

"Did you really get a bear?"

Without the skins we could not satisfy them. But how they knew that we were coming or why they had expected us on Wednesday was something I have never yet discovered.

* * * * * *

The next morning Pete phoned me at the office.

"Hello."

"Hello."

"Can you hear me?"

"No. Speak into the mouth piece."

"How's that?"

"Better."

"Just thought I'd call up to say hello and tell you I am going to New Hampshire this afternoon for the week end."

"Good, I am going to Cape Cod. How are you going?"

"Train. How about you?"

"I'm taking the 12:30," I replied.

"Aren't you flying?"

"No, you poor fish, I know when I've had enough."